MEXICO
THE BEAUTIFUL
COOKBOOK

One hundred best recipes by
SUSANNA PALAZUELOS

Text by
MARILYN TAUSEND

Photography by
IGNACIO URQUIZA

CollinsPublishersSanFrancisco
A Division of HarperCollins*Publishers*

Published in the U.S.A. in 1994 by
Collins Publishers San Francisco
1160 Battery Street San Francisco, CA 94111 USA

Conceived and produced by Weldon Owen Inc.
814 Montgomery Street San Francisco, CA 94133 USA

President: John Owen
Publisher: Jane Fraser
Project Editor: Ruth Jacobson
Editor: Janet Mowery
Editorial Assistant: Kim Green
Index: Ken DellaPenta
Design and Art Direction: John Bull
Design Layout: Ruth Jacobson
Color Illustration: Nicole Kaufman
Black and White Illustrations: Neil Shigley
Production: James Obata, Stephanie Sherman
Food Stylists: Laura Caraza, Mónica Patiño,
Kay Mendieta de Alonso
Prop Stylists: Mariana Hagerman, Constanza Linares
Photography Assistant: René Lopez

ISBN 0-00-255464-X

The Beautiful Cookbook® series is a
registered trademark of Weldon Owen Inc.

Production by Mandarin Offset, Hong Kong
Printed in Hong Kong

Above: A Maya woman heads home with her daily supply of *masa*.
Pages 4–5: Chichén Itzá, in the northern Yucatan peninsula, was a sacred center for the Mayas and,
later, the Toltecs. Beyond the serpent head and the reclining *chacmool* lies the famous pyramid, El Castillo.
Pages 8–9: The mazelike configuration of Guanajuato, an old silver-mining town.

CONTENTS

INTRODUCTION

Until recently, most average food lovers thought of Mexican cooking in terms of *tacos, tamales* and tongue-scorching *salsas*. Few were aware of the exquisite *moles* and *pipianes* with their sauces of ground pumpkin seeds and spices, or the naturally "cooked" *ceviche*, a medley of raw seafood marinated in lime juice. Nor did they know that the soul-satisfying cup of hot chocolate they happily sipped on a cold winter day was a gift of the cacao and vanilla of Mexico's first civilizations.

But Mexican cooking is more than indigenous dishes journeying untouched through the centuries. It is the grafting of the fruits and vegetables, meats, grains and spices of the Old World onto the root stock of the native foods, resulting in a cuisine that reflects its turbulent evolution through the centuries—crêpes of exotic corn fungus, bowls of steaming *menudo*, pit-roasted pork seasoned with *achiote* and bitter orange, and, yes, the uncountable varieties of *tacos, tamales* and *salsas,* shockingly hot to the unprepared palate.

From the beginning, corn has been central to the cuisine of Mexico. Nomadic hunters discovered that they could obtain a life-sustaining food by dropping a tiny kernel of maize in the dirt, nurturing it, bringing in the harvest, preparing it and finally eating it. These farmers forged a pattern of culture that would continue for nearly three thousand years.

With the arrival of the Spaniards came the ingredients and memories of a cuisine infused by twenty-eight generations of Moorish control. Livestock, poultry, wheat, rice, onions, garlic, citrus fruit and sugar cane found an accepting home in the new land. Their culinary merger with foods used by the native Indians—especially *chile,* chocolate and vanilla—changed the taste of foods eaten around the world.

Think how dull an Indian curry would be without *chiles* to give it life—or a Hungarian goulash without paprika. It is said that in Hunan, people can live without meat but not without hot pepper. Imagine Italian food without the Mexican contribution. There would be no pizza or spaghetti without tomatoes; no German chocolate cake; no American turkey and pumpkin pie.

In 1981 distinguished women chefs from Mexico formed the Círculo Mexicano de Arte Culinario, dedicated to preserving, enhancing and promoting the regional dishes of Mexico. Those cooks, and others, have contributed recipes to this book, sharing both traditional dishes and new interpretations. The recipes cover the spectrum of Mexican cooking, from the ubiquitous *frijoles de la olla*—the pot of beans found simmering in almost every Mexican kitchen—to the elegant lobster and pine nut crêpes served in the sophisticated restaurants of Mexico City.

Enjoy, and *buen provecho!*

SEAFOOD IN COCONUT SHELLS (RECIPE PAGE 85)

ANTOJITOS Y BEBIDAS

ANTOJITOS are the foods of the street and the marketplace, eaten out of hand during all hours of the day. Most are made of a centuries-old source of nourishment—*masa,* a dough of ground dried corn and water.

The tortilla is the bread, the plate and the spoon of Mexico. With cheese it becomes a *quesadilla.* Simple but exquisite. Filled *tacos;* layered *tostadas;* stuffed *gorditas* and *panuchos; sopes* and *garnachas;* the more elaborate *enchiladas*—the choice is endless and each region has its own specialties.

For every special occasion in Mexico, there are *tamales,* the food of fiestas. Unadorned and unaccompanied, filled or unfilled, wrapped in corn husks, fresh leaves of corn or banana or the large, pungent leaves of *hierba santa,* this steamed *masa* offering is served as a gift to the gods.

Where *antojitos* are eaten, close by are giant jars of *aguas frescas*—cooling beverages of blended fruit pulp. Two of the favorites are also the most unusual: *agua de tamarindo,* made from the sticky pod of the tamarind tree, and the ruby red *agua de jamaica,* made from the hibiscus blossom.

According to legend, Quetzalcóatl, the god of light, came to earth to help the impoverished Toltec Indians.

As he came to know and love these people, he taught them how to grow cacao and prepare chocolate, the sacred drink of the gods.

Pulque, the original Mexican alcoholic beverage, is the naturally fermented sap of the maguey, or century plant, grown on the high plateaus. It is often tempered with blended fruits to balance the spicy foods it usually accompanies. The hard-drinking Spaniards roasted, crushed and fermented the huge (80–200 pound) pineapple-shaped hearts of smaller species of maguey to produce the potent and popular mescal and tequila.

One of Mexico's many brands of beer or *agua mineral* usually shares the table with the food. With more than 300 springs in the country, mineral water has long been a popular beverage in Mexico. The country produces a variety of beers that are known and prized throughout the world.

A cup of rich, fragrant coffee usually ends the meal. Most people order the dark-roasted bean served *con leche* (with milk). The traditional but harder-to-find *café de olla,* brewed in a large earthenware pot (*olla*) and infused with cinnamon bark and dark brown sugar, is worth the search.

Bebidas and *antojitos* are all savored and appreciated as a meaningful part of the Mexican cycle of life.

ENCHILADAS POTOSÍ STYLE (RECIPE PAGE 21) AND MARGARITAS (RECIPE PAGE 13)

QUESO FUNDIDO CON CHAMPIÑONES Y RAJAS DE POBLANO

MELTED CHEESE WITH MUSHROOMS AND CHILE POBLANO STRIPS

Queso fundido is featured along with grilled cabrito (baby goat) around Guadalajara and across the northern states of Mexico, where it may be called queso flameado. The stringy melted cheese is served in shallow clay or metal dishes and scooped up with floppy flour tortillas. A spicy tomato salsa is added right before eating. This recipe uses mushrooms and chile poblano strips, but fried and crumbled chorizo is another delicious possibility.

1 *chile poblano,* roasted (see glossary), peeled
    and cut into strips (about ½ cup)
2 tablespoons (1 oz/30 g) butter
salt and freshly ground pepper
3 oz (60 g) mushrooms, sliced
2 cups (8 oz/250 g) grated mild Cheddar or
    Monterey Jack cheese
10–12 flour tortillas

Sauté the *chile* strips in 1 tablespoon butter, season with salt and pepper and set aside.
Sauté the mushrooms in the other tablespoon of butter until they begin to release their juices. Season with salt and pepper and set aside.
Lightly grease 2 *cazuelitas* or small flameproof casseroles. In one, place half the cheese and half the *chile* strips. In the other, place the remaining cheese and half the mushrooms. Cover the *cazuelitas* with aluminum foil and set over low heat until the cheese begins to melt, about 3 minutes. Uncover and cook another 2 minutes or until the cheese is completely melted. Add the remaining mushrooms and *chile* strips to their respective *cazuelitas.*
Serve hot with flour tortillas, so that the cheese can be used in preparing individual tacos. Can also be served with *salsa mexicana* (page 97).

Serves 6

MELTED CHEESE WITH MUSHROOMS, CHILE POBLANO STRIPS AND CHORIZO

MARGARITAS

MARGARITAS

The best known cocktail in Mexico is the margarita, first made in a Chihuahua bar.

4 cups (32 fl oz/1 l) or more crushed ice
½ cup (4 fl oz/125 ml) white tequila
¼ cup (2 fl oz/60 ml) cointreau
juice of 4 limes

1½ teaspoons salt

▦ In a blender, whirl the ice, tequila, cointreau and lime juice for 30 seconds.
▦ Moisten the rim of 6 glasses with lime juice and invert on a saucer of salt to lightly coat the rims with salt. Divide the margarita mixture among the glasses and serve.

Serves 6   *Photograph page 10*

TORTILLAS DE MASA HARINA
TORTILLAS MADE WITH MASA HARINA

Masa harina (literally, "dough flour"), a unique kind of flour or meal made from corn, can be thought of as dried masa. *Although neither corn flour nor cornmeal can be substituted,* masa harina *is widely available in the United States under the Quaker brand.*

2 cups (8 oz/250 g) *masa harina*
1½ cups (12 fl oz/375 ml) lukewarm water
(approximately)

🔲 *Note:* Keep a small bowl of lukewarm water nearby as you work to moisten your hands.
🔲 Place the *masa harina* in a large bowl and add the lukewarm water, mixing with your hands to incorporate the flour and form a ball. Cover with a cloth and let stand for 5–10 minutes.
🔲 Heat a *comal* or iron skillet (ungreased). Knead the dough for 2–3 minutes, then form into balls about the size of a walnut.
🔲 Cover a tortilla press with a sheet of plastic wrap and place a ball of dough in the center. Place another sheet of plastic wrap on top, lower the top lid of the press and push down on the handle. The tortilla formed should be 4½–5 in (10–13 cm) in diameter. If you are making *picaditas* or *quesadillas,* only press the handle halfway down, to form a tortilla about 3 in (7.5 cm) in diameter.
🔲 Open the tortilla press and remove the top sheet of plastic wrap from the tortilla. Lift the tortilla using the bottom sheet and turn it over onto your hand. Peel off the bottom sheet of plastic wrap and place the tortilla on the hot *comal.* Be careful not to "toss" the tortilla onto the *comal* or skillet because that would trap air and prevent it from cooking evenly.

🔲 As soon as the edges of the tortilla start to dry out, after about 20 seconds, turn it over. Cook the second side for 15–20 seconds and turn the tortilla again. After about 15 more seconds, remove the tortilla from the heat. Transfer to a cloth so that the tortillas can be kept covered.

Makes about 10 Tortillas

Nayarit

TEPACHE
FERMENTED PINEAPPLE DRINK

A refreshing fermented beverage made from Mexico's native pineapple and popular in many regions of the country.

1 whole ripe pineapple, about 3 lb (1.5 kg)
12 cups (96 fl oz/3 l) water
20 oz (600 g) *piloncillo* (raw sugar) or brown sugar
1 3-in (7.5-cm) stick cinnamon
3 whole cloves

🔲 Wash the pineapple thoroughly, remove the stem and cut into large pieces, rind and all.
🔲 Place the pineapple chunks in a large bowl and add 8 cups (64 fl oz/2 l) of the water and the *piloncillo,* cinnamon stick and cloves. Cover and let stand in a warm place for 48 hours.
🔲 Strain the *tepache* and add 4 cups (32 fl oz/1 l) water. Or, if you prefer, add 1 cup (8 fl oz/250 ml) of beer (lager) and let stand an additional 12 hours, then strain and add 3 cups (24 fl oz/750 ml) water. Serve cold, with ice cubes.

Serves 6   *Photograph page 23*

PANELA CHEESE WITH OREGANO

Jalisco

QUESO PANELA CON ORÉGANO

PANELA CHEESE WITH OREGANO

Panela *is a fresh white cheese known for its versatility. It can be eaten alone, as a dessert with slices of* ate *(fruit paste) or in this flavorful way combined with oil and oregano.*

1 lb (500 g) *queso panela* (or *queso fresco* or
   fresh mozzarella cheese)
6 cloves garlic, crushed
⅓ cup (3 fl oz/80 ml) olive oil
½ cup (4 fl oz/125 ml) corn oil
2 tablespoons ground oregano

Place the cheese in an earthenware or ovenproof dish. Pierce the outside of the cheese with a fork.

In a small bowl, combine the garlic, olive oil, corn oil and oregano until they are thoroughly blended. Pour over the cheese. Refrigerate, covered, for at least 4 hours, preferably overnight. During this time, baste the cheese with the oil 3 or 4 times.

Preheat the oven to 350°F (180°C). Bake the cheese for 15 minutes or until slightly soft. Serve warm with crackers or sliced *bolillos* (hard bread rolls).

Serves 6

GUACAMOLE
AVOCADO DIP

In the language of the Aztecs, the combined words for "avocado" and "mixture" translate into guacamole—*a wonderful concoction that is perfect served with* tacos or botanas *(before-meal snacks). In Mexico,* guacamole *is still made with the traditional* molcajete *and* tejolote *(mortar and pestle) or with a fork and bowl. A food processor or blender should not be used because the mixture should have a chunky texture. Although hard avocados are best ripened at room temperature in a paper sack, one should not overlook the advice of a Mexican adage: "Avocados and girls are ripened with squeezes."*

2 large avocados
1 tablespoon finely chopped onion
1 or 2 *chiles serranos,* sliced
1 large tomato, peeled and chopped
2 sprigs *cilantro* (coriander), chopped
lime juice
salt

Cut the avocados in half, remove the pits and scoop out the flesh. Mash with a fork.
In a bowl or *molcajete,* combine the avocado, onion, *chiles,* tomato and *cilantro* and mix thoroughly. Add a few drops of lime juice and salt to taste. Serve immediately.

Serves 6

PORK AND CHICKEN TAQUITOS (RECIPE PAGE 22) SERVED WITH GUACAMOLE

PANUCHOS DE CAZÓN

SHARK IN TORTILLA POCKETS

There are many versions of these panuchos, *or stuffed tortillas, a specialty of the Yucatán peninsula. They are also simply referred to as* pan de cazón *(shark's bread). If small dogfish shark is unobtainable, another meaty white fish such as mackerel can be substituted.*

SHARK

1 lb (500 g) shark steaks or mackerel fillets
3 bay leaves
4 cloves garlic, 2 whole, 2 minced
¼ onion
1 tablespoon oil
½ cup (4 oz/125 g) diced onion
1 lb (500 g) tomatoes, finely chopped,
   with peel and juice
2½ tablespoons chopped *epazote*
1 teaspoon dried oregano
salt and freshly ground pepper

RED ONIONS

2 tablespoons oil
1 lb (500 g) red onions, sliced
2 cloves garlic
½ cup (4 fl oz/125 ml) white vinegar
¾ cup (6 fl oz/180 ml) water
3 bay leaves
1 small sprig thyme
1 small sprig marjoram
1 teaspoon dried oregano
1 teaspoon salt
¼ teaspoon freshly ground pepper

oil for frying
12 corn tortillas

1 cup (8 oz/250 g) *frijoles refritos* (page 96)
pickled chiles serranos

▦ Heat 2 cups (16 fl oz/500 ml) water in a saucepan. When it comes to a boil, add the shark, 1 bay leaf, the whole garlic cloves and the onion quarter. Cover and cook over high heat for 20 minutes. Set aside.

▦ In a large skillet, heat the oil and add the diced onion and minced garlic. Sauté for 1 minute, then add the tomatoes. Stir and cook over medium heat for 3 minutes or until the tomato changes color. Add the *epazote,* 2 bay leaves and oregano and season with salt and pepper. Cover and cook over low heat for 2 minutes.

▦ Drain the shark and crumble it (not too finely). Add it to the skillet and cook over high heat for 2 minutes. Lower the heat and cook another 5 minutes, stirring constantly. Set aside.

▦ To prepare the red onions, in a nonreactive (not aluminum) saucepan, heat the oil, add the onions and sauté lightly. Add the garlic and sauté for 1 minute. Add the vinegar, water, bay leaves, thyme, marjoram, oregano, salt and pepper. Cook, uncovered, for 10 minutes or until the onions are soft. Correct the seasonings and set aside.

▦ Place 1 in (2.5 cm) oil in a large skillet. When it is hot, add a tortilla and fry until it puffs up. Remove the tortilla with a skimmer and, while it is still warm, carefully make a small horizontal opening in it, being sure not to pierce the other side. Repeat this procedure with all the tortillas.

▦ Carefully place a spoonful of *frijoles refritos* in the "pocket" you have made in each tortilla. Transfer the tortilla to a platter and

SHARK IN TORTILLA POCKETS

arrange some cooked shark and a layer of red onions on top of the *panucho*. Garnish with the pickled *chiles serranos*.

■ *Note:* If you are unable to open a pocket in the tortilla or if the tortilla does not puff up, you can take a lightly fried tortilla, spread it with beans, cover with another tortilla, then arrange the shark and red onions on top.

Serves 6

GREEN CHILAQUILES

CHILAQUILES VERDES O ROJOS
GREEN OR RED CHILAQUILES*

The Aztecs combined their leftover tortillas with chiles *and herbs to create* chilaquiles, *which in their Náhuatl language means just that— "chiles and herbs in broth." Every Mexican cook seems to have their own version of this versatile dish, which can be served either for* almuerzo *(brunch) or* cena *(supper).* Chilaquiles *can be prepared ahead up to the point of adding the sauce to the fried tortilla pieces.*

1 whole chicken breast, about 12 oz (375 g)
5 cloves garlic
1 tablespoon plus 1 teaspoon salt

½ onion
7 sprigs parsley
6 *chiles serranos* (or to taste)
1½ lb (750 g) *tomates verdes,* husks removed
¼ onion
½ cup (¾ oz/20 g) chopped *cilantro*
   (coriander)
1 tablespoon oil
16 corn tortillas, preferably day-old
oil for frying
1 small sprig *epazote*
1 cup (8 fl oz/250 ml) thick cream
   (*crème fraîche*)
½ cup (2 oz/60 g) crumbled *queso fresco*
   or *queso añejo* (or feta cheese)

▓Place the chicken in a large saucepan and add enough water to cover. Add 2 cloves of the garlic, 1 tablespoon of the salt, ½ onion and the parsley. Cover and simmer for 20 minutes or until the chicken is tender. Remove and shred the chicken, reserving 2 cups (16 fl oz/500 ml) of the stock.
▓Place the *chiles* and remaining 3 cloves garlic in boiling water and cook for 5 minutes. Add the *tomates verdes,* cook 5 more minutes and drain. Transfer the *chiles,* garlic and *tomates verdes* to a blender, add the remaining onion, then purée. Add 1 teaspoon salt, the *cilantro* and 1 cup (8 fl oz/250 ml) of the reserved stock, and process briefly. Set aside.
▓Heat 1 tablespoon oil in a skillet, add the sauce and sauté for 5 minutes. Correct the seasonings, lower the heat, cover and cook for 10 minutes. If the mixture is too thick, dilute with more chicken stock.
▓Cut the tortillas in half and cut each half into 3 pieces. Place ¼ in (1 cm) oil in a large

skillet. When it is very hot, add one-third of the tortilla pieces and fry, stirring constantly, until they are golden and crisp, 3 to 4 minutes. Transfer to a colander. Repeat until all the tortillas are fried. Drain and set aside.

▦ Before serving, heat the sauce and add the *epazote*. Add the tortillas and stir carefully so as not to break them. Add the shredded chicken and top with cream and cheese. Cook for 2–3 minutes or until the cheese melts.

★ Chilaquiles Rojos: *To make red chilaquiles, substitute 1½ lb (750 g) ripe tomatoes for the tomates verdes. Instead of boiling, roast the tomatoes (see glossary), peel and then purée with the boiled chiles.*

Serves 6 as main course, 8 as first course

San Luis Potosí

ENCHILADAS POTOSINAS
ENCHILADAS POTOSÍ STYLE

These unusual enchiladas, with red chile ground in the masa, are sold from small stands in the industrial capital of San Luis Potosí. More like a quesadilla in appearance, they are usually served with shredded lettuce and guacamole (page 17).

2½ oz (75 g) *chiles anchos*, seeds and
  membranes removed
1 cup (8 fl oz/250 ml) hot water
1 tablespoon lard
1 tablespoon oil
¼ cup (2 oz/60 g) minced onion
1¼ cups (5 oz/155 g) crumbled *queso fresco*
  (or feta cheese)

1 lb (500 g) *masa*
½ teaspoon salt
oil for frying

▦ Toast the *chiles* (see glossary) and soak in the hot water for 25 minutes, then purée in a blender with ½ cup (4 fl oz/120 ml) of the water in which they soaked. Melt the lard in a small skillet, add the *chile* purée and sauté for 5 minutes. Set aside.

▦ Heat the oil in a small skillet, add the onion and sauté until it is transparent. Remove from the heat and stir in the cheese. Add 1 tablespoon of the *chile* purée and stir well. Set aside.

▦ Place the *masa* in a bowl, add the remaining *chile* purée and the salt and knead for 5 minutes or until all the ingredients are thoroughly combined. Cover with a damp cloth and let rest for 20 minutes.

▦ Form the *masa* into balls about the size of walnuts, place between 2 pieces of plastic wrap in a tortilla press, and flatten to form circles about 3 in (7.5 cm) in diameter. Remove the plastic. Spread a tablespoon of the cheese mixture in the middle of each circle, leaving a narrow margin. Fold the circles in half and press the edges to seal.

▦ Heat a *comal* or iron skillet and toast the *enchiladas* for 2 or 3 minutes on each side or until the *masa* changes color and seems cooked. (The *enchiladas* can be prepared in advance up to this point and refrigerated for up to 3 hours.) Heat ½ in (1 cm) oil in a skillet, add the *enchiladas* 2 or 3 at a time and fry for 3 or 4 minutes on each side. Drain and serve.

Makes 12 Enchiladas   *Photograph page 10*

TAQUITOS DE PUERCO O POLLO

SMALL TACOS WITH PORK OR CHICKEN

Tacos date from early Indian civilizations, when stews were eaten rolled up in tortillas. They are now enjoyed everywhere in Mexico—at any time and with almost any filling imaginable. It is said that the taquero, *the man who sells tacos, is always the first to arrive at any spectacle.*

1 lb (500 g) boneless cubed pork or chicken
3 black peppercorns
1 clove garlic, peeled
salt
4 cups (32 fl oz/1 l) water
3 tablespoons chopped *cilantro* (coriander)
1 onion, chopped
20 corn tortillas
oil for frying

▧ Place the pork, peppercorns, garlic and 1 teaspoon salt in a saucepan, add the water and bring to a boil. Lower the heat so that the mixture simmers and cook, covered, for 35 minutes or until the pork is tender. Let cool, then shred the meat.

▧ Mix the *cilantro* with the chopped onion and season with a little salt. Add the shredded pork.

▧ Place a large spoonful of the meat mixture in the center of each tortilla, roll up and secure with 2 toothpicks. Slice each *taco* in half.

▧ Heat ½ in (1 cm) oil in a skillet, add the *taquitos* and fry until they are golden brown. Remove the toothpicks and serve the *taquitos* as a snack, accompanied by *guacamole* (page 17) and *salsa de tomate verde con aguacate* (page 94).

Serves 6–8   *Photograph page 17*

ENCHILADAS VERDES

GREEN ENCHILADAS

According to Renato Luduc, the writer and poet from the state of Aguascalientes, "After the cock fights, after card games, there is no Aguascalientes visitor or family member who doesn't go on to savor a plate of chicken enchiladas or some other regional dish at the stands lined up alongside the beautiful gardens of San Marcos."

1 whole chicken breast, about 12 oz (375 g)
6 cups (48 fl oz/1.5 l) water
5 cloves garlic
1 small onion (4 oz/125 g), ½ cut in half,
    ½ thinly sliced
3 small sprigs parsley
salt
1 carrot, cut into large pieces
2–4 *chiles serranos*
2 lb (1 kg) *tomates verdes,* husks removed
½ cup (¾ oz/20 g) coarsely chopped *cilantro*
    (coriander)
1 tablespoon oil
12 corn tortillas
oil for frying
½ cup (4 fl oz/125 ml) thick cream
    (crème fraîche) (optional)
½ cup (2 oz/60 g) crumbled *queso fresco* or
    grated Cheddar cheese (optional)

▧ Place the chicken, water, 3 cloves garlic, ¼ onion, parsley, salt to taste and carrot in a large saucepan, cover and simmer until the chicken is tender, about 20 minutes. Remove and shred the chicken, reserving the stock.

▧ Add 2 cloves garlic and the *chiles* to a large

GREEN ENCHILADAS AND FERMENTED PINEAPPLE DRINK (RECIPE PAGE 15)

saucepan of boiling water. After 5 minutes, add the *tomates verdes* and cook for another 7 minutes. Drain.

⊞ In a blender, purée the *tomates verdes* with the garlic, *chiles* and another onion quarter. Add the *cilantro* and process briefly so that the *cilantro* is not ground too fine. Add 1 cup (8 fl oz/250 ml) of the reserved chicken stock.

⊞ Heat the oil in a small skillet and sauté the puréed *tomates verdes* in it. Add 1 teaspoon salt and correct the seasonings. Lower the heat and cook, uncovered, for 10 minutes. If the sauce is too thick, add another ½ cup (4 fl oz/250 ml) stock.

⊞ Heat ½ in (1 cm) oil in a skillet and fry the tortillas in it until they just begin to soften,

10 seconds on each side. Immerse each tortilla in the warm sauce, then transfer to a plate. Place some chicken in the center of each tortilla, roll up and arrange on a platter. Spoon the warm sauce over the *enchiladas*, garnish with the sliced onion and add cream and *queso fresco* if you wish.

⊞ *Variation:* The *enchiladas* can be placed in an oven-proof dish, covered with sauce, wrapped in aluminum foil and placed in a preheated oven (375°F/190°C) for 10 minutes. Remove from the oven, sprinkle with Cheddar cheese and return to the oven until the cheese browns slightly.

Serves 6

QUESADILLAS

QUESADILLAS

The authentic quesadilla *is made with an uncooked tortilla that is stuffed, folded over and cooked on a comal.* Cheese with a sprig of epazote *is the classic filling, but popular variations include mushrooms, potatoes with chorizo, or squash flowers; see following recipes. It is important that these be served the moment they are cooked.*

1 lb (500 g) *masa*
3 tablespoons all-purpose (plain) flour
1 tablespoon melted lard
1 teaspoon baking powder (optional)
½ teaspoon salt
oil for frying

Place the *masa* in a large bowl and add the flour, lard, baking powder and salt. Moisten your hands and knead for 5 minutes. Cover with a damp cloth and let rest for 10 minutes.

Form the *masa* into 12 balls. Line a tortilla press with plastic wrap, place a ball of *masa* in the center and cover with another piece of plastic. Press lightly to form 4-in (10-cm) circles. Peel the plastic from the top of the

QUESADILLAS WITH POTATO AND CHORIZO FILLING, CHEESE FILLING AND SQUASH BLOSSOM FILLING

tortilla and spread a spoonful of filling (recipes follow) on the tortilla in a half circle, leaving a ½-in (1-cm) margin around the edge. Fold the tortilla in half and remove the plastic from the bottom. Press the edges of the *quesadilla* to seal.

In a skillet, heat ½ in (1 cm) oil to 375°F (190°C). Fry the *quesadillas,* 2 at a time, for 2 or 3 minutes on each side or until lightly browned. Do not let them stick together as they fry.

Serve with *guacamole* (page 17) and *salsa mexicana* (page 97).

Makes 12 Quesadillas

RELLENO DE QUESO
CHEESE FILLING

1 cup (4 oz/125 g) grated *queso manchego, queso Oaxaca,* Monterey Jack or Muenster cheese
small sprigs *epazote* (optional)

Place a spoonful of cheese and a sprig of *epazote* in each *quesadilla.*

Makes 1 cup (4 oz/125 g)

RELLENO DE PAPA CON CHORIZO
POTATO AND CHORIZO FILLING

2½ cups (13 oz/410 g) peeled and cubed potatoes
1 *chorizo* (5 oz/155 g) or other spicy sausage, casing removed and chopped

Cook the potatoes in boiling salted water. When they are tender, drain and place in a bowl. Mash slightly with a fork.

Heat a skillet, add the *chorizo* and cook over low heat for 8 to 10 minutes.

Add the *chorizo* to the potatoes. Moisten with a tablespoon of the fat rendered from the *chorizo* and mix well.

Makes about 2½ cups (1¼ lb/625 g)

RELLENO DE FLOR DE CALABAZA
SQUASH BLOSSOM FILLING

2½ cups (5 oz/155 g) squash (zucchini) blossoms or 1 can (7 oz/220 g) squash (zucchini) blossoms, drained
1 tablespoon oil
½ cup (4 oz/125 g) finely chopped onion
1 clove garlic, minced
1 tomato (6 oz/185 g), peeled and finely chopped
¼ cup (3 oz/90 g) diced *chile poblano,* seeds and membranes removed
1 tablespoon chopped *epazote*
1 teaspoon salt

Remove the stems and pistils from the flowers. Rinse with water, drain and chop the flowers coarsely.

Heat the oil in a skillet, add the onion and garlic and sauté for 2 minutes. Add the tomato, stir and heat for 3 minutes or until the mixture comes to a boil. Add the flowers, *chile poblano, epazote* and salt. Cook, uncovered, over medium heat until the flowers are soft and the excess liquid has evaporated, about 4 minutes.

Makes about 2½ cups (1¼ lb/625 g)

FRESH CORN TAMALES AND CAFÉ DE OLLA

Michoacán

UCHEPOS

FRESH CORN TAMALES

For some reason these delicate fresh corn tamales of Michoacán are never quite the same when prepared elsewhere, but they still are unique and very good. In Mexico they would be made with fresh field corn, which has a higher starch content. The best substitute is corn that has been picked for several days and is not too sweet or tender.

8–10 ears (cobs) corn
⅓ cup (3 fl oz/80 ml) milk
2 tablespoons sugar
½ teaspoon salt
2 tablespoons softened butter or lard

Use a sharp knife to slice through the thick end of the corn ears. Remove the husks, being careful not to break them, and set aside. Slice the kernels off the cobs; you should have about 5 cups (20 oz/625 g). Place the kernels in a bowl. Moisten your hands and use them to stir the kernels so that any corn silk sticks to your hands and can be removed.

Place 1 cup of the corn kernels in a blender and process at high speed, adding milk as necessary. Do not process too thoroughly; the mixture should be the consistency of cottage cheese. Repeat until all the corn has been processed.

Stir in the sugar and salt and mix well. Add the softened butter or lard and combine thoroughly.

Place the steamer basket in a steamer and add hot water up to ½ in (1 cm) below the bottom of the basket. Line the basket with the stiffer corn husks.

Take a pliable corn husk, spread it out and place a tablespoon of the filling in it. Roll up the husk loosely and fold the point over the seam. Stack the prepared *tamales* in the steamer basket with their seams and points facing up, being careful not to crush them.

Cover with another layer of corn husks and place the lid on the steamer. When the water comes to a boil, reduce the heat to low and cook for 1 hour or until the filling inside a husk appears curdled.

Let the tamales cool for at least 20 minutes so that they dry and the filling does not stick to the husks.

The *tamales* can be served rolled in the husk or unrolled and placed 2 on a plate with a little *salsa de molcajete* (page 94) and a tablespoon of *crème fraîche*. Or they can be served by themselves.

Note: The *tamales* can also be cooked in a pressure cooker. After the steam escapes, close the valve and cook for 20 minutes.

Serves 14–16

CAFÉ DE OLLA
COFFEE IN A CLAY POT

For this popular after-supper drink, coffee, sugar, cinnamon and spices are simmered in a clay pot to produce a most distinctive flavor that is best appreciated when served in small clay mugs. For best results, use a coarsely ground, dark-roasted coffee like a Viennese roast.

5 cups (40 fl oz/1.25 l) water
½ cup (2 oz/60 g) coarsely ground
   dark-roasted coffee
4 oz (125 g) *piloncillo* (raw sugar)
1½ 4-in (10-cm) sticks cinnamon
5 whole cloves
peel from ¼ orange

Heat 4 cups (32 fl oz/1 l) of the water in an *olla* or small saucepan over moderate heat. When it comes to a boil, lower the heat and add the coffee, *piloncillo*, cinnamon sticks, cloves and orange peel. Simmer for 5 minutes.

Add 1 cup (8 fl oz/250 ml) cold water, remove from the heat and cover. Let stand for 5 minutes. Strain before serving.

Serves 6

SOPAS

RED, GREEN AND WHITE, the colors of Mexico's flag, are also the colors of its *pozoles,* the country's most famous all-in-one-dish meal. All are redolent of the flavor of long-simmered pork and thick with hominy, but there the similarity ends. In Guerrero green *pozole* is made with fresh *chiles,* greens, ground pumpkin seeds and tangy little *tomates verdes.* Each dish is further embellished with finely chopped onion, crispy *chicharrón* (crisp-fried pork rinds), cubes of avocado, fresh oregano and a squeeze of lime.

In Jalisco, the simple, hunger-satisfying dish *pozole blanco* (white *pozole*) comes into its own. Pieces of pork, including the head, simmer with the hominy in an earthenware pot throughout the day. At the time of eating, a dose of ground *chile piquín* or an equally pungent *salsa* is added, along with chopped radishes, lettuce or cabbage. The result is a delicious layered meal of meat, starch and vegetable.

In Michoacán, fragrant pots of simmering broth give promise of the rich taste of *chile ancho* and *chile guajillo.* This deep-red soup, *pozole rojo,* is served with the characteristic oregano topping of Guerrero. Variations of all three *pozoles* can be found in each of these states as well as in other parts of Mexico.

Caldo de pollo, mole de olla, clemole and *menudo* are other popular soups served as a complete meal. *Menudo,* a comforting soup of tripe, is commonly eaten the morning after a night of alcoholic indulgence. It is said that the high vitamin B content accompanied by the fiery bite of *chiles* gives a person back his zest for living.

Soups are a relatively new addition to the Mexican table. None of the early Spanish chronicles mentions soups; the closest dish would be the thick stews the Indians cooked in large clay *ollas.* Today, first-course soups include the simple *sopa de fideo* (noodle soup), the wonderful *sopa de tortilla* (tortilla soup), the more unusual *sopa de médula* (a rich meat broth full of tasty pieces of mouth-melting bone marrow) and the exotic *sopa de cuitlacoche.* The fungus *cuitlacoche,* which grows in dark globular masses on ears of corn, has a flavor fit for royalty.

In the mid-sixteenth century the galleons that sailed from the Philippines to Acapulco and Barra de Navidad brought the first rice to the New World. In the convents and kitchens of the Spanish aristocracy, native cooks combined it with tomatoes, *chiles* and herbs, or even with fried bananas. It was served as a *sopa seca,* or "dry soup"— a transitional dish between the starter and the main course.

Sopas secas may also be crêpes, soufflés, pasta or even a thick vegetable *budín* (pudding). With their mild flavors, *sopas secas,* are a delicious surprise to those new to the varied flavors of Mexican cooking.

CLAM SOUP MADE WITH FRESH CLAMS IN THEIR SHELLS (RECIPE PAGE **32**)

SOPA DE TORTILLA

TORTILLA SOUP

If just one soup could be labeled the classic Mexican soup, it would probably be this one, combining as it does the traditional flavors and textures of the country's chile, tomato, avocado, epazote and tortilla.

3 cloves garlic
½ onion, cut into chunks
3 ripe tomatoes
6 cups (48 fl oz/1.5 l) chicken stock
   (page 32)
1 tablespoon oil
2 small sprigs *epazote*
salt and freshly ground pepper
8–10 day-old corn tortillas
oil for frying
2–3 *chiles pasillas*
2 avocados, peeled, pitted and chopped
5 oz (155 g) *queso fresco* (or feta cheese),
   crumbled
½ cup (4 fl oz/125 ml) thick cream
   (*crème fraîche*)
3 limes, halved

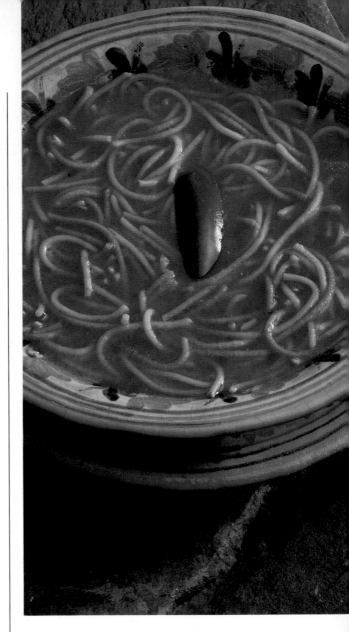

Roast the garlic, onion and tomatoes (see glossary). Peel and core the tomatoes and purée in a blender with the garlic and onion, adding ¼ cup (2 fl oz/60 ml) of the chicken stock if necessary.

Heat 1 tablespoon oil in a large saucepan over high heat and sauté the tomato purée. Boil for 2 minutes, lower the heat and cook, stirring constantly, for another 5 minutes or until the purée thickens and changes color.

Add the remaining chicken stock and *epazote*. Return to a boil, add salt and pepper to taste and cook, covered, over medium heat for 15 minutes.

Cut the tortillas in half and cut each half into thin strips. Heat ½ in (1 cm) oil in a small skillet and, when hot, add the tortilla pieces a few at a time and fry, turning at least once, for about 3 minutes or until golden brown.

PASTA SOUP (LEFT, RECIPE PAGE 34) AND TORTILLA SOUP (RIGHT)

Remove from the oil with a slotted spatula and drain on absorbent paper. (If using fresh tortillas, dry first in a preheated 250°F/120°C oven for an hour.)

Cut the *chiles* into ½-in (1-cm) rings and remove their seeds. Fry in the hot oil for about 1 minute or until crisp. Drain and set aside.

Five minutes before serving, reheat the soup and add the fried tortilla strips. Garnish each bowl of soup with a few *chile* rings and the avocado. Sprinkle with the cheese. Pass the cream, lime halves and remaining *chile* rings and avocado in separate bowls so that each person can add them to taste.

Serves 6

Baja California Norte

SOPA DE ALMEJAS

CLAM SOUP

This soup would most likely have been made from the sweet pismo clams of Ensenada, but any other fresh clams could be used instead of canned. The recipe is unusual in that it does not contain any chiles.

3 tablespoons olive oil
¾ cup (6 oz/185 g) chopped onion
2 cups (12 oz/375 g) chopped celery
1 clove garlic, minced
3 cups (1 lb/500 g) peeled and cubed potatoes
8 cups (64 fl oz/2 l) chicken stock
   (recipe follows)
salt
2 cans (15 oz/470 g each) chopped clams,
   drained, with juice reserved
1½ cups (2 oz/60 g) finely chopped parsley
juice of 1 lime

▨ Heat 1 tablespoon of the oil in a large pot or Dutch oven, add the onion, celery and garlic and cook for 5 minutes or until transparent. Add the potatoes, chicken stock and 1 cup (8 fl oz/250 ml) of the clam juice and simmer, covered, over low heat for 15 minutes or until the potatoes are tender. Add salt to taste. ▨ Ten minutes before serving, bring the broth to a boil and add the chopped clams. Return to a boil and add the chopped parsley, remaining olive oil and lime juice. Serve immediately.

Serves 6   *Photograph page 28*

CALDO DE POLLO

CHICKEN STOCK AND SOUP

Eaten everywhere in Mexico, this simple, nourishing soup is often served as a main course. The vegetables may vary, but it is almost always served with lime, chopped onions and green chiles. Chicken stock is a major ingredient in many recipes, so it is wise to make it in advance and freeze it. It can be frozen in ice cube trays, and the cubes stored in plastic bags. Chicken parts such as the back and neck can also be used.

STOCK
1 whole chicken, about 3 lb (1.5 kg), cut
   into serving pieces
10 cups (80 fl oz/2.5 l) water
1 whole carrot
4 cloves garlic
1 tablespoon salt
6 black peppercorns
1 small sprig parsley
1 small onion, quartered

SOUP
¼ cup (2 oz/60 g) canned or cooked
   chickpeas
1 *chayote* (vegetable pear/choko), peeled
   and quartered
1 large potato, peeled and cut into
   chunks
2 ears (cobs) corn, each cut into 3 pieces
2 carrots, thickly sliced
1 cup (3 oz/90 g) sliced cabbage
2 sprigs *cilantro* (coriander)
1 sprig spearmint
1 cup cooked rice (about 2 oz/60 g uncooked)
   (optional)
3 limes, sliced

CHICKEN SOUP

4 *chiles serranos,* seeds and membranes removed, and chopped

½ cup (4 oz/125 g) chopped onion

⊞ To make the stock, rinse the chicken and giblets and place in a large pot or Dutch oven. Add the water, whole carrot, garlic, salt, peppercorns, parsley and onion. Bring to a boil, skim the surface, cover and cook over medium heat for 1 hour. Let cool, remove the chicken and degrease the stock.

⊞ To make the soup, add the chickpeas after the stock has cooked for only 30 minutes.

Cook 30 more minutes, then discard the parsley, onion and whole carrot. Add the *chayote,* potato, corn, sliced carrots, cabbage, *cilantro* and spearmint. Cover and cook over medium heat for 30 minutes or until the vegetables are tender.

⊞ To serve, put a piece of chicken and some vegetables in each bowl, add some rice if you like and pour the hot broth over. Pass the lime slices and chopped *chiles* and onion separately.

Serves 6–8

SOPA DE PASTA
PASTA SOUP

Pasta arrived in Mexico during the thirty years of Porfirio Díaz's presidency, with its emphasis on grand continental cuisine. This recipe calls for fideos, *or vermicelli, but almost any soup pasta can be used, even stars, wheels or alphabet types. The trick is to have the noodle acquire the proper light-brown color without getting too dark and bitter tasting.*

2 tomatoes
¼ onion
2 cloves garlic
½ cup (4 fl oz/125 ml) water
2 tablespoons oil
1 package (8 oz/250 g) vermicelli or other thin pasta
8 cups (64 fl oz/2 l) chicken stock (page 32)
salt
chiles serranos (optional)

In a blender, purée the tomatoes, onion and garlic with the water. Strain and set aside.
Heat the oil in a large saucepan or Dutch oven, add the pasta and stir until it begins to brown. Pour off the excess oil. Add the puréed tomatoes and boil for 3 minutes, stirring constantly. Add the stock and bring to a boil. Cover and cook over medium heat for 10 to 15 minutes or until the pasta is tender. Add salt to taste. If you wish, garnish with the *chiles.*

Serves 6   *Photograph pages 30–31*

Guerrero

SOPA DE CALABACITAS
ZUCCHINI SOUP

Zucchini, a favorite for Mexican creamed soups, is spectacularly served inside a round squash.

3 lb (1.5 kg) zucchini (courgettes), cut into chunks
4 cups (32 fl oz/1 l) milk
2 cups (16 fl oz/500 ml) chicken stock (page 32)
3 tablespoons (1½ oz/45 g) butter
1 tablespoon minced onion
1½ teaspoons salt
½ teaspoon freshly ground pepper
6 acorn or other round squash (optional)

Cook the zucchini in a covered saucepan with a little water for 20 minutes or until they are crisp-tender. Drain.
In a blender, purée the zucchini, milk and stock. Melt the butter in a large saucepan, add the onion and sauté until transparent. Add the zucchini mixture, salt and pepper. Simmer, covered, over low heat for 5 minutes.
If you like, slice the tops off the squash, scoop out the flesh and serve the soup in these shells instead of large bowls.

Serves 6

ZUCCHINI SOUP

MELON SOUP (LEFT) AND CREAM OF AVOCADO SOUP (RIGHT)

Michoacán

CREMA DE AGUACATE

CREAM OF AVOCADO SOUP

The beautiful evergreen avocado tree is native to Mexico. Its fruit has long been prized by the Indians, and the early Spaniards savored its buttery texture and rich flavor. The Haas variety, so popular in California, originated in Atlixco in the state of Puebla, but this soup is from Uruapan in the hot country of Michoacán.

3 avocados, pitted and peeled
1 tablespoon lime juice
7 cups (56 fl oz/1.75 l) chicken stock
   (page 32)

pepper, then purée until smooth. If the soup is too thick, add another cup (8 fl oz/ 250 ml) of broth. Cover and refrigerate until well chilled.

▦ Just before serving, stir in the cream and correct the seasonings. If you like, sprinkle chopped *cilantro* on each serving.

Serves 6

Michoacán

SOPA DE MELON
MELON SOUP

Starting a meal with a cool fruit soup is an untraditional but highly satisfactory prelude to a main dish such as pechugas en salsa de poblano gratinadas *(page 60). Using a very ripe melon gives the soup a better flavor.*

3 cantaloupes (rock melons)
2 tablespoons honey
¼ cup (2 fl oz/60 ml) fresh lemon juice
½ cup (4 fl oz/125 ml) fresh orange juice
¼ cup (2 fl oz/60 ml) port

▦ Cut the cantaloupes in half, remove and discard the seeds, then scoop out the pulp, being careful not to tear the peel. Set the 6 cantaloupe shells aside.

▦ Roughly chop the cantaloupe pulp and purée in a blender with the honey, lemon juice, orange juice and port.

▦ Chill well before serving. Use the cantaloupe shells as soup bowls.

Serves 6

1 tablespoon chopped *cilantro* (coriander)
1 teaspoon salt
⅛ teaspoon freshly ground pepper
½ cup (4 fl oz/125 ml) thick cream (*crème fraîche*)

▦ Place the avocados in a blender along with the lime juice, chicken stock, *cilantro,* salt and

1 *chile poblano*
1 green bell pepper (capsicum)
3 tablespoons (1½ oz/45 g) butter
½ cup (4 oz/125 g) chopped onion
5 cups (40 fl oz/1.25 l) chicken stock
    (page 32)
2 tablespoons all-purpose (plain) flour
2 tablespoons cornstarch (cornflour)
¾ cup (6 fl oz/180 ml) water
4 cups (32 fl oz/1 l) evaporated milk
1 teaspoon salt
1 teaspoon freshly ground pepper
4 oz (125 g) *queso Chihuahua* (or Monterey
    Jack or medium-sharp Cheddar cheese),
    finely chopped (about 1 cup)
1 cup (8 oz/250 g) chopped tomato

Remove the stems, seeds and membranes from the *chile* and bell pepper and cut into a small dice; there should be about 1¼ cups.
Melt 1 tablespoon of the butter in a skillet, add the onion and sauté for 2 minutes or until transparent. Add the *chile* and bell pepper and cook for 3 minutes. Set aside.
Bring the stock to a boil in a large saucepan. Stir the flour and cornstarch into the water, add to the stock and stir constantly for 2 minutes. Add the milk and lower the heat. When it comes to a boil, add the bell pepper and *chile* and cook over low heat for 5 minutes. Add the salt and pepper and cook 2 minutes more. Add the remaining 2 tablespoons butter (1 oz/30 g) and set aside.
Before serving, heat the soup and place 2 tablespoons of cheese and 2 tablespoons of tomato in the bottom of each bowl.

Serves 8

CHEESE SOUP

Sonora

SOPA DE QUESO
CHEESE SOUP

In some parts of Sonora, potato chunks are added to this typical regional soup. If queso Chihuahua *is not available, use Monterey Jack or a medium-sharp Cheddar.*

Distrito Federal

CALDO TLALPEÑO
SOUP TLALPEÑO STYLE

This smoky-flavored soup comes from old Tlalpan, once an area of beautiful haciendas and now a bustling Mexico City suburb. As in many Mexican dishes, a squeeze of lime brings out the taste.

1 whole chicken breast, about 12 oz (375 g)
6 cups (48 fl oz/1.5 l) chicken stock
   (page 32)
1 cup (8 oz/250 g) cooked or canned
   chickpeas
2 cloves garlic
1 tablespoon oil
⅔ cup (5 oz/155 g) chopped carrots
½ cup (4 oz/125 g) chopped onion
2 pickled *chiles chipotles*, seeded and cut
   into strips
1 small sprig *epazote*
salt
1 avocado, peeled, pitted and cubed
2 tablespoons chopped *cilantro* (coriander)
   (optional)
lime slices
1 ripe tomato, chopped
2 *chiles serranos*, finely chopped
1 cup cooked rice

■ Place the chicken, stock, chickpeas and garlic in a large saucepan and cook, covered, over medium heat for 20 minutes or until the chicken is tender. Transfer the chicken to a plate and, when cool enough to handle, remove the meat from the bones, shred and set aside.
■ Heat the oil in a skillet, add the carrots and onion and sauté for 3 minutes. Transfer to the pot of chicken stock and add the *chiles, epazote* and salt to taste. Cook, covered, for 30 minutes over low heat. Correct the seasonings.
■ Place a few cubes of avocado and some shredded chicken in each soup bowl. Fill with hot soup and sprinkle with *cilantro* if desired. Serve the lime separately. Pass the tomato, *chiles* and rice in small bowls so that everyone can add to their soup as much as they want.

Serves 6–8

SOUP TLALPEÑO STYLE

POZOLE

PORK AND HOMINY SOUP

The original white pozole is said to have been created in Chilapa, Guerrero, during the eighteenth century on the occasion of a visit by an important prelate from Puebla. Legend has it that local cooks prepared enormous quantities of nixtamal (softened dried corn kernels) days in advance, but there were not enough people to grind the maize and make tortillas. In desperation, maize was thrown into pots with chicken and herbs, and thus pozole, now a revered national dish, was born. In Jalisco and Michoacán is found a pozole rojo, rich red with chiles. Chiles anchos can be substituted or combined with the chiles guajillos. Pozole verde's green hue and unusual taste and texture comes from ground pumpkin seeds, tomates verdes and various greens. All versions of pozole are usually served with lime sections.

1 whole chicken, about 3 lb (1.5 kg),
    cut up
½ onion
3 cloves garlic
4 teaspoons salt
1 sprig *cilantro* (coriander)
cold water
2 lb (1 kg) boneless lean pork
1 lb (500 g) boneless pork butt (pork leg)
2 lb (1 kg) dried hominy, cooked and
    drained
3 oz (90 g) dried oregano
1 cup (8 oz/250 g) chopped onions
3 oz (90 g) ground *chile piquín*
5 limes, halved

▦ Place the chicken in a large pot or Dutch oven and add the onion, garlic, 1 teaspoon of the salt and the *cilantro.* Cover with 10 cups (80 fl oz/2.5 l) water, bring to a boil and simmer, covered, over medium heat for 20 minutes or until the chicken is tender. Transfer the chicken to a plate, remove the skin and bones and shred the meat. Reserve the stock. There should be about 8 cups (64 fl oz/2 l).

▦ Place the pork, pork butt and remaining salt in a large pot and cover with 14 cups (112 fl oz/3.5 l) water. When the water comes to a boil, skim the surface and cook over medium heat for 1 hour. Add the hominy and cook another 30 minutes. Remove and shred the meat and return it to the pot.

▦ Add the chicken stock and shredded chicken to the pot, correct the seasonings, cover and cook over medium heat for 20 minutes or until the hominy is tender.

▦ Serve in small earthenware bowls and pass separate dishes containing the oregano, chopped onion, *chile piquín* and lime halves.

Serves 12

POZOLE ROJO

RED POZOLE

10–12 *chiles guajillos,* seeds and membranes
    removed
½ cup (4 fl oz/125 ml) water
¼ onion
4 cloves garlic
7 tablespoons oil

Soak the *chiles* in hot water to cover for 20 minutes, then drain. In a blender, purée the *chiles* with the water, onion and garlic.

Heat the oil in a skillet over high heat, add the *chile* purée and sauté for 5 minutes. Lower the heat and cook for 10 minutes.

Add this sauce to the *pozole* when you mix in the shredded chicken and pork.

about 3 minutes, stirring constantly. Add the puréed *tomates verdes* and boil for 2 minutes. Add the salt, lower the heat and cook, stirring constantly, for 7 minutes. Correct the seasonings.

Add this sauce to the *pozole* when adding the shredded chicken and pork.

WHITE POZOLE (TOP), GREEN POZOLE (CENTER) AND RED POZOLE (BOTTOM)

POZOLE VERDE
GREEN POZOLE

2 cups (8 oz/250 g) hulled raw
    pumpkin seeds
3 *chiles serranos*
1 lb (500 g) *tomates verdes,* husks removed
2 leaves lettuce
3 small radish leaves
¼ onion
½ cup (4 fl oz/125 ml) chicken stock
    (page 32)
2 tablespoons oil
1 teaspoon salt

Toast the pumpkin seeds in a skillet until they begin to pop, being careful that they do not burn. Transfer them to a blender and grind to obtain a smooth paste. Set aside.

Bring a large saucepan of water to a boil, add the *chiles* and cook for 5 minutes. Add the *tomates verdes* and cook for 3 minutes. Drain and set aside.

In a blender, purée the *tomates verdes, chiles,* lettuce, radish leaves and onion with the chicken stock. Set aside.

Heat the oil in a large casserole or skillet. Add the pumpkin seed paste and sauté for

ARROZ A LA MEXICANA
MEXICAN-STYLE RICE

In Mexico, rice dishes are often served as a separate course, as a dry soup (sopa seca) replacing the more usual liquid one. During the years when the wealthy entertained lavishly on their haciendas, both types of soups were presented at the same meal. Whenever the phrase a la mexicana is used, as in this popular way to fix rice, the dish has been prepared with onions and tomatoes.

2 cups (10 oz/315 g) long-grain white rice
2 tomatoes
¼ cup (2 fl oz/60 ml) oil
⅓ onion, chopped
3 whole cloves garlic
4 cups (32 fl oz/1 l) chicken stock (page 32) or water
1 small sprig parsley
3 whole *chiles serranos* (optional)
½ cup (4 oz/125 g) chopped carrot
¼ cup (1 oz/30 g) shelled green peas

▦ Soak the rice for 5 minutes in warm water, rinse well and drain. Meanwhile, purée the tomatoes in a blender and strain.

▦ Heat the oil in a skillet, add the onion and garlic and sauté for 2 minutes. Add the rice and sauté, stirring, until translucent and the grains separate. Pour off excess oil.

▦ Add the puréed tomatoes to the skillet with the rice. Cook for 4 minutes and add the stock, parsley, *chiles,* carrot and peas. When the mixture comes to a boil, cover and cook over medium heat for 20 minutes or until the liquid has been absorbed and the rice is tender.

Serves 6

MEXICAN-STYLE RICE

CUITLACOCHE CRÊPES WITH POBLANO SAUCE

Distrito Federal

CREPAS DE CUITLACOCHE CON SALSA DE POBLANO

CORN FUNGUS CRÊPES WITH POBLANO SAUCE

This intriguing marriage of French crêpes with Mexican corn fungus was first served in the court of Emperor Maximilian and his wife, Carlotta. It is a very distinguished dish for special occasions.

CRÊPES
2 cups (16 fl oz/500 ml) milk
1 small egg
1 cup (4 oz/125 g) plus 1 tablespoon all-purpose (plain) flour
1 tablespoon oil
butter

FILLING
2 tablespoons (1 oz/30 g) butter

⅓ cup (3 oz/90 g) finely chopped onion
1 *chile poblano,* seeds and membranes removed and diced
½ cup (2 oz/60 g) corn kernels
1 tablespoon chopped *epazote*
2 cans (7 oz/220 g each) *cuitlacoche* or 5 oz (155 g) fresh *cuitlacoche*

SAUCE
2 *chiles poblanos,* seeds and membranes removed
⅓ cup (3 fl oz/80 ml) milk
¼ cup (2 oz/60 g) butter
1½ tablespoons all-purpose (plain) flour
2 cups (16 fl oz/500 ml) thick cream *(crème fraîche)*
1 teaspoon salt
1½ cups (6 oz/185 g) grated *queso Chihuahua* (or Monterey Jack or medium-sharp Cheddar cheese)

▦ To prepare the crêpes, in a mixing bowl, beat together the milk, egg, flour and oil. Let rest for 5 minutes. Lightly butter a nonstick crêpe pan and set over medium heat. Pour 1½ tablespoons of the batter into the pan and tilt it to cover the bottom. As soon as the edges of the crêpe begin to dry out, turn it over. When the second side is lightly browned, transfer the crêpe to a plate. Repeat until all the batter has been used. There should be about 22 crêpes. Set aside.

▦ To prepare the filling, melt the butter in a skillet, add the onion and sauté for 2 minutes or until transparent. Add the *chile,* corn, *epazote* and *cuitlacoche* with its juice. Cook over medium heat for 5 minutes, stirring constantly.

▦ To prepare the sauce, purée the *chiles* in a blender with the milk. Melt the butter in a small saucepan. Add the flour and cook, stirring constantly, until it is lightly browned.

Remove from the heat and continue to stir while adding the cream, *chile* purée and salt. Return to low heat and stir constantly until the sauce begins to boil. Set aside.

▨To assemble, place a tablespoon of filling on each crêpe, roll up and cut off the uneven edges. Arrange in a single layer in a greased ovenproof dish. Cover with aluminum foil until 15 minutes before serving.

▨Before serving, preheat the oven to 500°F (260°C). Pour the sauce over the crêpes and sprinkle with the cheese. Bake for about 10 minutes or until the cheese begins to melt. Or place in the broiler (griller) until the sauce bubbles and the cheese is lightly golden.

Serves 8

Distrito Federal

BUDÍN AZTECA

AZTEC CASSEROLE

A layered casserole similar to chilaquiles *(page 20),* budín Azteca *makes a perfect main course for today's lighter eaters and is best with a crispy salad. The chicken can be omitted for a vegetarian meal, or pork can be substituted. It is often called* budín Cuauhtemoc *or* budín Moctezuma.

2 tablespoons oil
½ cup (4 oz/125 g) chopped onion
2 cloves garlic, finely chopped
3 large tomatoes (1½ lb/750 g), peeled and puréed
1½ teaspoons salt
1 tablespoon butter
3 cups (12 oz/375 g) fresh or frozen corn kernels
20 oz (625 g) zucchini (courgettes), chopped
⅓ cup (3 fl oz/80 ml) water
oil for frying
10 corn tortillas
2 *chiles poblanos,* roasted (see glossary), peeled, membranes removed and cut into strips
1 cup (8 fl oz/250 ml) thick cream *(crème fraîche)*
1 cup (5½ oz/170 g) cooked and shredded chicken
1 cup (4 oz/125 g) grated *queso manchego* (or Muenster, Monterey Jack or white Cheddar cheese)

▨Heat the oil in a skillet, add the onion and garlic and sauté until transparent. Add the tomatoes and salt and cook over high heat for 5 minutes. Lower the heat, cover and cook for 10 more minutes. Correct the seasonings and set aside.

▨Preheat the oven to 375°F (190°C). Melt the butter in a saucepan. Add the corn and zucchini and cook for 2 minutes. Add the water, cover and cook over low heat for 8 minutes or until the zucchini is crisp-tender.

▨Heat ½ in (1 cm) oil in a skillet and fry the tortillas for 30 to 40 seconds on each side, just to soften. Set aside.

▨Place a thin layer of the vegetables on the bottom of a greased baking dish, top with a layer of 4 or 5 tortillas, then add a layer of the tomato sauce. Add half the remaining vegetables, half the *chiles,* ½ cup (4 fl oz/125 ml) of the cream, half the chicken and ½ cup (2 oz/60 g) of the cheese. Repeat the layers, finishing with the cheese. Bake, uncovered, until the cheese begins to melt, 10–15 minutes. Remove from the oven and serve.

Serves 6–8   *Photograph pages 46–47*

FOLLOWING PAGES: AZTEC CASSEROLE (LEFT) AND SQUASH BLOSSOM SOUP (RIGHT, RECIPE PAGE 48)

Tlaxcala

SOPA DE FLOR DE CALABAZA
SQUASH BLOSSOM SOUP

Squash blossoms can be found in the Mexican markets during the early morning and are most abundant during the rainy season from June to October. You can also find them fresh (in season) or canned at specialty stores outside of Mexico. It is advisable to cook them as soon as possible, as they are very delicate and stay fresh for a brief period.

2 lb (1 kg) squash (zucchini) blossoms
7 tablespoons (3½ oz/105 g) butter
3 green (spring) onions, thinly sliced
6 cloves garlic, slivered
6 *chiles serranos,* thinly sliced
¼ teaspoon each dried marjoram, thyme
    and tarragon
1 tablespoon chopped parsley
salt and freshly ground pepper
8 cups (64 fl oz/2 l) chicken stock (page 32)
1 boneless chicken breast, about 8 oz (250 g),
    skin removed and cut into ½-in (1-cm) cubes
⅓ cup (1½ oz/45 g) sliced mushrooms
2 cups (16 fl oz/500 ml) thick cream (*crème fraîche*)

▦Remove the stems and pistils from the blossoms. Rinse gently, shaking off the excess water. Chop coarsely and set aside.
▦Melt ¼ cup (2 oz/60 g) of the butter in a large skillet. Add the green onions, garlic and *chiles*. Sauté lightly and add the squash blossoms. Stir for 2 minutes and add the marjoram, thyme, tarragon and parsley. Season with salt and pepper and cook, covered, for 3 minutes.
▦Heat the chicken stock in a large saucepan and add the flower mixture. Cook, covered,

over low heat for 5 minutes. Set aside.
▦Meanwhile, in a skillet over medium heat, sauté the chicken in 3 tablespoons (1½ oz/45 g) of butter until golden. Set aside.
▦Add the chicken and mushrooms to the hot stock. Correct the seasonings and stir in the cream. Serve piping hot.

Serves 6   *Photograph pages 46–47*

Oaxaca

LENTEJAS CON FRUTA
LENTILS WITH FRUIT

Lentils, long favored in Old World cuisines, are too often neglected by today's cooks. In this dish, the ancient legume's earthy qualities are complemented by the smoky pork and sweet fruit flavors.

2 cups (12 oz/375 g) dried lentils
8 cups (64 fl oz/2 l) water
8 oz (250 g) bacon, chopped
8 oz (250 g) *longaniza, chorizo* or other spicy
    sausage, casings removed and cut into
    chunks
1 cup (8 oz/250 g) chopped onion
2 cloves garlic, minced
2 slices fresh pineapple, chopped
1 plantain or large firm banana, about
    12 oz (375 g), peeled and sliced
1 teaspoon salt
½ teaspoon freshly ground pepper
6 small green (spring) onions
2 tablespoons oil
4 smoked pork chops
1 lb (500 g) blood sausage (black pudding),
    cut into chunks (optional)

LENTILS WITH FRUIT

Place the lentils and water in a large saucepan and bring to a boil. Lower the heat and simmer, covered, for 45 minutes. If you need to add more water, be sure that it is hot. Drain the lentils, reserving the cooking liquid.

In a large saucepan, sauté bacon over medium heat for 2 minutes. Add the *longaniza* and cook, covered, for 3 minutes. Add the onion and garlic and sauté for 3 minutes. Add the lentils, pineapple, plantain, salt and pepper and cook, covered, over low heat for 10 minutes. Add 2 cups (16 fl oz/500 ml) of the liquid in which the lentils cooked and the green onions;

cover and cook over low heat for 30 minutes.

While they are cooking, heat the oil in a skillet. Add the smoked pork chops and sauté for 3 minutes on each side. Transfer to a plate. In the same oil, sauté the blood sausage for 2 minutes. Add the chops and blood sausage to the pan with the lentils and cook, covered, for 5 minutes.

Note: This should not be a soup but rather a lentil casserole. If you prefer it less thick, add 1 cup (8 fl oz/ 250 ml) water.

Serves 6–8

CARNES, AVES Y HUEVOS

IRONICALLY, the pre-Columbian Indians of Mexico ate the kind of high-fiber, low-cholesterol, low-fat diet espoused today by doctors—mainly fish and vegetables.

But the diet of the Indians was quickly and profoundly changed when the Spaniards introduced livestock to the New World. Chickens, goats and pigs soon became important food sources for the Indians.

A visit to the meat stalls of any Mexican market will reveal just how completely the pig is utilized. The head is used in the earthy *pozole* (hominy soup) or made into *queso de puerco* (head cheese). The tubelike intestines are stuffed with flavorful meat fillings and made into *chorizo* and *longaniza* (sausages), or filled with herb-seasoned blood and transformed into *moronga*. The innards are usually fried for the day's *tacos*.

Even all the fat of the pig is used—to make a favorite *botana* (snack), the crackly *chicharrón*, and for lard which is still considered indispensable in preparing *tamales* and *frijoles*.

In the northern border states, high-quality beef is king. However, in much of Mexico range-fed cattle, often Brahmas, are still raised, which are tough by any standard. Their meat is sliced with the grain into large thin sheets, tenderized by lime juice and quickly seared.

In Mexico today, even in the poorest households, the noble turkey can be seen strutting in dirt yards, and each market day finds them tethered among seated vendors or carried upside down by their feet, passive and unregal, on display for buyers anticipating the next fiesta, for turkey is the food of celebrations.

The chickens used in Mexican cooking are almost always free-range chickens and can be seen scratching along the sides of roads, eating whatever their pecking procures. The result is a chicken that has flavorful but tough meat that needs to be simmered or slowly braised to bring out its best.

Eggs are eaten everywhere, at any time and in many guises. They may be prepared as *huevos a la mexicana* laced with the colorful green *chiles serranos,* tomatoes and slices of onion, or scrambled with spicy *chorizo* or cooked pieces of *nopales* (cactus paddles).

The classic Mexican egg dish is *huevos rancheros,* fried eggs placed on soft-cooked tortillas, slathered with a coarse *picante* tomato sauce and paired with refried beans.

Eggs also are fried and layered for *tortas* (sandwiches) or used as a topping for a rice course. And on every restaurant cart of *postres,* the rich convent dessert *huevos reales* (royal eggs) from Puebla is a classic offering.

PORK ROAST STUFFED WITH CHILES CHIPOTLES
AND PRUNES (RECIPE PAGE 78)

BUTTERFLY QUAIL

Guerrero

CODORNIZ A LA TALLA

BUTTERFLY QUAIL

Quail was a bird prized by the Aztecs for eating and as a sacrifice to the goddess Chicomecóatl. In this method of cooking, a Guerrero specialty, the meat or fish is first coated with mayonnaise, then basted with a tongue-tingling sauce during grilling.

¼ cup (2 fl oz/60 ml) mayonnaise
1 tablespoon oil
1 teaspoon salt
½ teaspoon freshly ground pepper
12 quail or squabs, about 4 oz (125 g) each

SAUCE
10 *chiles guajillos*, seeds and membranes removed
5 *chiles anchos*, seeds and membranes removed
5 large ripe tomatoes
1 cup (8 fl oz/250 ml) water
4 cloves garlic
3 whole cloves
¼ large onion
1 tablespoon red wine vinegar
½ teaspoon each dried thyme, oregano and marjoram
½ teaspoon ground cumin
¼ cup (2 oz/60 g) butter

2 tablespoons oil
salt and freshly ground pepper

▧Combine the mayonnaise, oil, salt and pepper in a small bowl.

▧With a sharp knife, cut through each quail breast and press the bird open in a butterfly shape. Coat both sides of each quail liberally with the mayonnaise mixture and marinate at room temperature for at least 1 hour.

▧To prepare the sauce, cover the *chiles* with hot water and let soak for 20 minutes. Meanwhile, in a blender, purée the tomatoes, strain and set aside. Drain the *chiles,* then purée with the water, garlic, cloves, onion, vinegar, thyme, oregano, marjoram and cumin until smooth.

▧Heat the butter and oil in a small saucepan. Add the puréed *chiles,* bring to a boil and add the tomatoes. When the sauce comes to a boil, lower the heat and simmer, covered, for 45 minutes to an hour or until the sauce thickens, stirring occasionally. Add salt and pepper to taste. Let cool to room temperature. Baste the quail with half the sauce and marinate, refrigerated, for at least 4 hours.

▧Preheat an outdoor grill and grease the rack lightly with oil. Coat the quail with half of the remaining sauce. Cook for 4–5 minutes on the breast side and 1–2 minutes on the bone side, basting constantly with the rest of the sauce, until the quail are cooked to the desired doneness.

Serves 6

Oaxaca

HUEVOS OAXAQUEÑOS

EGGS OAXACA STYLE

Variations of this egg dish—this one by Socorrito Zorrilla—are popular throughout the Isthmus of Tehuantepec. In Oaxaca, a handful of cooked nopales (cactus paddles) is often added.

2 lb (1 kg) tomatoes
6 cloves garlic
1 onion
3 *chiles de agua* or small *chiles poblanos*
10 eggs
½ cup (4 fl oz/125 ml) milk
salt
butter or oil
½ cup (¾ oz/20 g) chopped *epazote*

▧Roast the tomatoes, garlic and onion (see glossary). Chop very fine. Roast the *chiles* separately (see glossary), remove the membranes and cut into strips.

▧Beat the eggs with the milk and sprinkle with salt. Scramble the eggs in a lightly greased skillet until just set, stirring constantly.

▧Place a little butter or oil in a *cazuela* or deep skillet and fry the tomato sauce for 5 minutes. Stir in the *chile* strips and *epazote,* then add the eggs. Correct the seasonings.

▧This egg dish is usually served very hot, accompanied by *frijoles de la olla* (page 96) and hot corn tortillas.

Serves 6 *Photograph page 67*

Michoacán

POLLO EN CUÑETE
CHICKEN IN A CLAY POT

The traditional way to prepare this chicken dish is in a clay casserole dish covered with a sealing layer of masa. *Small bits of the corn mixture break off and add a thickening texture to the sauce. This modern version is much simpler to prepare.*

1 whole chicken, about 3 lb (1.5 kg),
   cut into serving pieces
11 cloves garlic, crushed
1 tablespoon coarse salt
1 teaspoon freshly ground pepper
2 tablespoons corn or vegetable oil
20 small new potatoes, peeled
¾ cup (6 fl oz/180 ml) red wine vinegar
⅓ cup (3 fl oz/80 ml) olive oil
2 teaspoons salt
6 bay leaves
2 tablespoons each dried thyme
   and marjoram
2 *chiles serranos* (optional)

▨ Rub the chicken with the garlic, salt and pepper and refrigerate for 2–4 hours.

▨ In a large skillet, heat the corn oil, sauté the chicken briefly and transfer to a *cazuela* or large pot. In the same oil, lightly brown the potatoes, remove and set aside. Add the vinegar to the skillet and bring to a boil, scraping up browned bits from the bottom of the skillet. Pour the vinegar through a strainer over the chicken.

▨ Add the olive oil, salt, bay leaves, thyme and marjoram to the chicken *cazuela*. Bring to a boil over high heat, cover and lower the heat. Every 10 minutes, uncover and stir. After 35 minutes, uncover, correct the seasonings and add the *chiles* and potatoes. Cover and cook over low heat until the potatoes are tender, about 15 minutes.

Serves 6

HUEVOS A LA MEXICANA
MEXICAN-STYLE SCRAMBLED EGGS

The two favorite egg dishes of Mexico, huevos rancheros *and* huevos a la mexicana, *are both imbued with the chiles, onions and tomatoes that give Mexican food its characteristic taste. The seeds and membranes of the chile can be removed for a less picante dish.*

1 tablespoon oil
1 tablespoon chopped onion
¾ cup (6 oz/185 g) chopped tomato
1 *chile serrano,* chopped
⅛ teaspoon salt
2 eggs

▨ Heat the oil in a skillet. Add the onion and sauté until transparent. Add the tomato, *chile* and salt and sauté over medium heat for 5 minutes.

▨ Lightly beat the eggs, add to the tomato sauce and stir gently. Cover and cook over medium heat for 2–3 minutes or until the eggs are set. Serve with hot corn tortillas.

Serves 1 *Photograph page 67*

PAVO EN FRÍO
COLD TURKEY

While the scrub and rain forests are still inhabited by wild turkeys, it is the descendants of the bird that the Maya Indians domesticated centuries ago that are used today for this cold buffet dish.

1 young turkey, about 7 lb (3.5 kg)
3 oz (90 g) cured ham, cut into strips
5 cloves garlic, slivered
2 avocado leaves, central vein removed
    and cut into strips
12 black peppercorns
1 tablespoon each ground cinnamon
    and nutmeg
1 teaspoon ground cloves
9 qt (9 l) water
½ head garlic
½ onion
1 tablespoon salt
1 cup (8 fl oz/250 ml) olive oil
4 cups (32 fl oz/1 l) white wine
1 large onion, quartered
2 oranges, sliced
½ cup (4 fl oz/125 ml) lime juice

DRESSING
¾ cup (6 fl oz/180 ml) red wine vinegar
1½ cups (12 fl oz/375 ml) olive oil
salt

▨ Make small slits with a knife all over the turkey and insert the ham, garlic, avocado leaves and peppercorns in them. Rub the turkey with the cinnamon, nutmeg and cloves and wrap it in a double thickness of cheesecloth or a piece of thin white cloth. Transfer to a large pot or Dutch oven and add the water, garlic, ½ onion and salt. Cover and simmer for 1½ hours. Drain, reserving the stock.

▨ Return the turkey and 8 cups (64 fl oz/2 l) of the stock to the pot and add the oil, wine, onion, orange slices and lime juice. Cover and cook over medium heat for 1 hour or until the turkey is tender, basting occasionally. Remove the turkey from the pot and let cool for 30 minutes. Remove the cheesecloth.

▨ To prepare the dressing, measure out 3 cups (24 fl oz/750 ml) of the liquid from the pot. Add the vinegar, oil and salt to taste and mix well.

▨ Remove the skin from the turkey. Slice the breast and the meat from the legs and thighs and arrange on a large platter. Cover with the dressing and refrigerate, covered, for at least 2 hours.

Serves 12–14   *Photograph pages 64–65*

POLLO PLAZA DE MORELIA
PLAZA DE MORELIA CHICKEN

While this complete chicken dinner can be found in the restaurants of Morelia, the colonial capital of Michoacán, it is usually bought from vendors in a small plaza several blocks from the main plaza.

1 chicken, about 3½ lb (1.75 kg), cut into
    serving pieces
4 cups (32 fl oz/1 l) water
2 sprigs parsley
4 cloves garlic
1 onion, halved
1 tablespoon salt

3 (1 lb/500 g) potatoes, peeled and cut into chunks

3 (12 oz/375 g) large carrots, peeled and cut into chunks

3 *chiles anchos*

5 *chiles guajillos*

2 cloves garlic

1 tablespoon lard or oil

oil or lard for frying

12 corn tortillas

5 oz (155 g) *queso fresco* (or feta cheese), crumbled

shredded lettuce

½ onion, thinly sliced

In a large covered saucepan, simmer the chicken in the water with the parsley, garlic, ½ onion and salt for 35 minutes or until tender. Drain, reserving the stock, and set aside. Meanwhile, in another large saucepan, cook the potatoes and carrots in boiling salted water until tender. Drain and set aside.

Remove the stems and seeds from the *chiles*. Toast (see glossary) on a *comal* or iron skillet, then soak in hot water to cover for about 20 minutes. Drain and transfer to a blender.

Roast the garlic and remaining ½ onion (see glossary). Add to the blender and purée with the *chiles* and ½ cup (4 fl oz/125 ml) of the reserved stock.

Melt the lard in a skillet until very hot. Add the *chile* purée and cook, stirring constantly, for 2 minutes. Add 1½ cups (12 fl oz/375 ml) of the reserved stock and cook over medium heat for 5 minutes. If the sauce becomes too thick, thin it with a little more stock.

PLAZA DE MORELIA CHICKEN

Before serving, heat 1 tablespoon oil in a skillet. Dip both sides of a tortilla in the *chile* sauce, transfer to the hot oil, fry briefly on both sides and transfer to a plate. Place some *queso fresco* in the center of the tortilla and roll up. Repeat for the remaining tortillas. In the same skillet, sauté the chicken pieces on all sides with the carrots and potatoes.

On each plate arrange a bed of shredded lettuce. Place 2 *enchiladas* and a piece of chicken on top of the lettuce. Arrange the vegetables on the side. Garnish with onion slices and sprinkle with the remaining *queso fresco*.

Serves 6

Estado de México

CLEMOLE CASTELLANO

CASTILLIAN DUCK

Clemoles can be substantial soups, or dishes with sauces lighter than moles. Alicia Gironella De' Angeli, a highly regarded Mexican cookbook author, has harmoniously combined duck in her clemole.

2 tablespoons (1 oz/30 g) butter

1 tablespoon oil

4 whole duck breasts, about 8 oz (250 g) each, cut in half

¾ cup (3 oz/90 g) pine nuts

¾ cup (3 oz/90 g) chopped walnuts

¾ cup (3 oz/90 g) chopped hazelnuts

3 *chiles anchos,* seeds and membranes removed

3 *chiles pasillas,* seeds and membranes removed

1 tablespoon *chile* seeds

¾ cup (3 oz/90 g) toasted breadcrumbs

6 cups (48 fl oz/1.5 l) duck or chicken stock (page 32)

3 tablespoons brown sugar or honey

4 avocado leaves, toasted and crumbled, or ½ teaspoon aniseed, lightly toasted (see glossary)

salt and freshly ground pepper

¼ cup (1 oz/30 g) pine nuts for garnish (optional)

▨ Heat the butter and oil in a large heavy skillet over medium heat, add the duck breasts and sauté until half of their fat has been rendered, about 3–4 minutes on each side. Set aside.

▨ In the duck fat, sauté the nuts, whole *chiles,* seeds and breadcrumbs over medium heat until lightly browned. Cool, then purée with enough stock to form a smooth sauce. Add the sugar and avocado leaves and simmer until the sauce thickens. Add salt and pepper to taste. Set aside.

▨ Finish cooking the duck breasts in a lightly oiled heavy skillet over medium-high heat. Cook the skin side first until golden brown, then turn the breasts over and cook for another 3 or 4 minutes.

▨ To serve, place each breast on top of a small amount of sauce, cover with more sauce and garnish with pine nuts if you like.

Serves 8

SALSA DE JALAPEÑOS Y ACEITUNAS PARA PATO

OLIVE AND JALAPEÑO SAUCE FOR DUCK

The first Spaniards planted grapevines and olive trees in Baja California. Sherry and olives make an appearance in this delicate recipe by Alicia Gironella De' Angeli. The sauce is an excellent accompaniment for sautéed duck breasts or for any recipe using duck.

2 tablespoons chopped onion

4 cloves garlic, chopped

1½ cups (12 fl oz/375 ml) dry sherry or dry white wine

¼ cup (2 fl oz/60 ml) olive oil

2 pickled *chiles jalapeños,* seeds and membranes removed

¾ cup (4 oz/125 g) pitted green olives

4 tablespoons minced parsley

white pepper

DUCK WITH OLIVE AND JALAPEÑO SAUCE (TOP) AND CASTILLIAN DUCK (BOTTOM)

1½ cups (12 fl oz/375 ml) duck or chicken stock (page 32)

▨ In a small saucepan, cook the onion and half the garlic in the sherry over low heat until the mixture has the consistency of marmalade.

▨ Heat 1 tablespoon of the oil in a skillet, add the *chiles,* olives and most of the parsley and sauté for 1–2 minutes. Stir in the onion and garlic mixture. Cook for 4 minutes over low heat. Remove and stir in some white pepper. Let cool.

▨ Purée this mixture in a blender, adding stock as needed. Strain.

▨ Pour the sauce over duck. Serve with corn kernels and mushrooms sautéed in oil with garlic and minced parsley.

Serves 4

CHICKEN BREASTS IN POBLANO SAUCE AU GRATIN

San Luis Potosi

PECHUGAS EN SALSA DE POBLANO GRATINADAS

CHICKEN BREASTS IN POBLANO SAUCE AU GRATIN

An abundance of chiles grow throughout this state. They are often combined with excellent local cheeses of cow's and goat's milk in rich creamy dishes like this one.

3 whole chicken breasts, about 12 oz
   (375 g) each
salt and freshly ground pepper

1 large *chile poblano*
¼ cup (2 fl oz/60 ml) milk
¼ cup (2 oz/60 g) butter
1 tablespoon all-purpose (plain) flour
1 cup (8 fl oz/250 ml) thick cream *(crème fraîche)*
6 tablespoons (1½ oz/45 g) grated Cheddar
   cheese

☙ Remove the bones and skin and cut each chicken breast in half. Flatten each half slightly and sprinkle with salt and pepper. Refrigerate for 20 minutes.

▦ Remove the stem, seeds and membranes from the *chile,* then purée in a blender with the milk.

▦ Melt 2 tablespoons (1 oz/30 g) of the butter in a small saucepan. Add the flour and stir until smooth. Add the *chile* purée and stir. Add the cream and stir constantly over low heat until the mixture boils and thickens. Remove from the heat and add salt to taste. (This sauce can be made up to 6 hours ahead and reheated over low heat before using.)

▦ Preheat the oven to 350°F (180°C). Melt the remaining 2 tablespoons butter in a skillet, add the chicken breasts and sauté for 2 minutes on each side. Transfer to a lightly greased small baking dish, cover with the *poblano* sauce, sprinkle with the cheese and bake for 10 minutes.

Serves 4–6

Tlaxcala

CAZUELITAS CON HUEVOS Y CHILES POBLANOS
EGGS AND POBLANO CHILES IN CAZUELITAS

Although this rich egg dish has traditional ingredients, María Dolores Torres Yzábal prepares them in an untraditional way to create a dish suitable for a first course or a light meal.

4 eggs
1½ cups (12 fl oz/375 ml) thick cream (*crème fraîche*)
¾ teaspoon salt
1½ cups (6 oz/185 g) grated *queso Chihuahua* (or Monterey Jack or medium-sharp Cheddar cheese)

2 large *chiles poblanos,* roasted (see glossary), seeds and membranes removed, and diced

▦ Preheat the oven to 350°F (180°C). In a mixing bowl, beat the eggs with a fork, adding the cream and salt a little at a time.

▦ Divide the cheese evenly among 6 *cazuelitas* or ramekins, top with the *chiles* and fill with the egg mixture.

▦ Place the *cazuelitas* in a hot-water bath and bake for 40 minutes or until set.

Serves 6

EGGS AND POBLANO CHILES IN CAZUELITAS

MOLE POBLANO DE GUAJOLOTE
TURKEY WITH POBLANO MOLE SAUCE

This legendary dish is said to have been created in seventeenth-century Puebla by Sister Andrea de la Asunción, a Dominican nun from the Santa Rosa convent, with the original recipe including more than one hundred ingredients. Today, mole *remains the classic dish for festive occasions such as weddings and baptisms. It is better to prepare the sauce in advance, adding the turkey when it is reheated—not only because of the work involved in preparing the* mole *but because it tastes better when the various flavors have time to mingle and mellow.*

1 young turkey, about 8 lb (4 kg), cut into
　serving pieces
16 cups (128 fl oz/4 l) water
4 cloves garlic
½ onion
1 tablespoon salt

SAUCE
½ cup (4 fl oz/125 ml) plus 2 tablespoons oil
7 oz (220 g) *chiles anchos,* seeds and membranes
　removed
3 oz (90 g) *chiles pasillas,* seeds and membranes
　removed
10 oz (315 g) *chiles mulatos,* seeds and
　membranes removed
4 *chiles chipotles*
1½ lb (750 g) tomatoes
1 onion, coarsely chopped
10 cloves garlic
5 oz (155 g) blanched almonds
3½ oz (105 g) shelled peanuts
8 whole cloves

4 black peppercorns
1 1½-in (4-cm) stick cinnamon
½ teaspoon aniseed
3 oz (90 g) raisins
3 oz (90 g) unsweetened (cooking)
　chocolate
1 tablespoon sugar
2 tablespoons salt, or to taste
½ cup (2 oz/60 g) sesame seeds

▧ Place the turkey, water, garlic, onion and salt in a large pot or Dutch oven, bring to a boil, cover and simmer over medium heat for 1 hour or until the turkey is tender. Drain, reserving the stock, and set aside.

▧ To make the sauce, heat 2 tablespoons of the oil in a skillet, add the *chiles anchos, pasillas* and *mulatos* and sauté for 1–2 minutes. Transfer to a bowl, cover with hot water and soak for 30 minutes. Drain, transfer to a blender and purée. Set aside.

▧ Toast the *chiles chipotles* and roast the tomatoes (see glossary). Peel the tomatoes, transfer to a blender, add *chiles chipotles* and purée. Set aside.

▧ In the same oil in which you sautéed the *chiles,* sauté the onion and garlic for 2–3 minutes. Transfer to a blender. In the same oil, sauté the almonds for 5 minutes. Add the peanuts, cloves, peppercorns, cinnamon and aniseed and sauté for 3 more minutes. Transfer to the blender, add the raisins and purée.

▧ Heat the remaining oil in a large pot or Dutch oven. Stir all of the purées together, add to the pot and boil for 5 minutes, stirring constantly. Add the chocolate and sugar, stirring constantly. When the mixture comes to a boil, add 4 cups (32 fl oz/1 l) of the turkey stock. Cover and

TURKEY WITH POBLANO MOLE SAUCE

cook over low heat for 20 minutes. Add the salt and correct the seasonings. If the sauce is too thick, add more stock.

Add the pieces of turkey, cover and cook over medium heat for 10 minutes. Meanwhile, toast the sesame seeds in a small skillet over medium heat until they are golden. Serve the *mole* hot, sprinkled with the sesame seeds.

Serves 10–12

POLLO EN ESCABECHE
MARINATED CHICKEN

The word escabeche *comes from the Arabic* sikiube, *which means "acid," and is a method for light pickling. In Mexico,* escabeches *combine wine or vinegar with citrus juices, bay leaves and other herbs. This Maya recipe also includes the traditional* achiote *paste, or* recado rojo, *which is available in some Hispanic markets or can be made.*

1 whole chicken, about 3 lb (1.5 kg), cut up
10 cups (80 fl oz/2.5 l) water
½ onion, roasted (see glossary)
4 cloves garlic, roasted (see glossary)
salt
3 sprigs *cilantro* (coriander)
2 teaspoons dried oregano
2 teaspoons ground cumin
4 cloves garlic, unpeeled
1 cup (8 fl oz/250 ml) orange juice
½ cup (4 fl oz/125 ml) lime juice or 1½ cups
   bitter (Seville) orange juice
1 lb (500 g) red onions, thinly sliced
1 teaspoon salt
6 *chiles cristal* or *chiles habaneros,* roasted
   (see glossary)

MARINADE
3 oz (90 g) *achiote* paste (page 67)
½ cup (4 fl oz/125 ml) orange juice
¼ cup (2 fl oz/60 ml) lime juice
1 tablespoon lard, melted and cooled

❋ Place the chicken, water, roasted onion and garlic, 1 tablespoon salt and the *cilantro* in a large pot or Dutch oven and cook, covered, over medium heat for about 30 minutes or until the chicken is tender. Drain and set aside.
❋ Meanwhile, toast the oregano, cumin and garlic (see glossary). Peel the garlic and purée in a blender with the oregano, cumin, orange juice and lime juice.
❋ Place the red onions in an earthenware or enamel container and add the purée. Stir, add 1 teaspoon salt and bring to a boil over

COLD TURKEY (LEFT, RECIPE PAGE 56) AND MARINATED CHICKEN (RIGHT)

medium heat. Remove from the heat, add the *chiles* and set aside for at least 2 hours.

To make the marinade, dissolve the *achiote* paste in the orange and lime juices in a small bowl. Baste each piece of chicken with this mixture and marinate at room temperature for 30 minutes to 1 hour. Baste all the chicken pieces thoroughly with the melted lard.

Preheat an outdoor grill and lightly grease the rack. Grill the chicken for 5 minutes on each side, let cool 5 minutes and shred the chicken. (This can also be done in an oven broiler.) To serve, arrange the shredded chicken on a large platter and cover with the red onions and *chiles*.

Serves 6–8

Oaxaca

HIGADITOS DE FANDANGO

FESTIVE CHICKEN

The name of this traditional fiesta recipe contributed by Socorrito Zorrilla literally means "little livers" but is confusingly composed of chicken (usually without livers) and eggs. Cooking in Mexico is not just a matter of taste and smell. In the simple Zapotec Indian kitchens of Oaxaca, the women rely mainly on their ears when preparing this dish. The secret comes from beating the eggs with a large sharp knife until the sound changes from "tlacawhup tlacawhup" to a thicker "whalcawhump."

1 chicken, about 3 lb (1.5 kg)
4 cups (32 fl oz/1 l) water
1 tablespoon salt
½ onion
2 cloves garlic
2 leaves *hierba santa* (optional)
8 eggs
6 tablespoons (3 oz/90 g) lard or oil
1 small onion, chopped
3 cloves garlic, minced
2 large tomatoes, seeded and chopped
4 *tomates verdes,* husks removed and chopped
1½ teaspoons ground cumin
2 peppercorns, ground
1 whole clove, ground
1 pinch saffron

▨ Place the chicken in a large pot or Dutch oven with the water, salt, onion, garlic and *hierba santa*. Bring to a boil, then cover and simmer for 35 minutes or until the chicken is tender. Drain, reserving the stock. When the chicken is cool enough to handle, shred the meat. You should have about 2½ cups (14 oz/440 g).

Beat the eggs thoroughly in a large bowl and gently stir in the shredded chicken.
▨ Melt the lard in a deep *cazuela* or large skillet. When it is hot, add the onion and garlic and sauté until transparent. Add the tomatoes and *tomates verdes* and sauté until tender—about 5 minutes—then add 2 cups (16 fl oz/500 ml) of the reserved stock and the ground spices. Bring to a boil, lower to a simmer and gradually pour in the chicken-egg mixture. Without stirring, cook the mixture over low heat until the eggs are set.
▨ With a spatula, loosen the sides so that the eggs do not stick to the pan and some of the sauce comes to the top. (There will be a solid egg mass sitting in the sauce.)
▨ Serve with a *chiles pasillas* sauce (below).

Serves 8

PASILLA CHILE SAUCE

1 tablespoon oil
4 *chiles pasillas,* seeds and membranes removed
1 clove garlic
1 teaspoon salt
⅔ cup (5 fl oz/160 ml) water
1 tablespoon white vinegar
½ teaspoon dried oregano

▨ In a skillet, heat the oil, add the *chiles* and sauté for 40 seconds, stirring constantly. Rinse. Transfer the *chiles* to a blender, add the garlic, salt and water and purée briefly. There should be pieces of roughly chopped *chile*. Transfer to a bowl, stir in the vinegar and oregano and serve with the *higaditos de fandango*.

Makes about 1½ cups (12 fl oz/375 ml)

FESTIVE CHICKEN (LEFT, SERVED WITH PASILLA CHILE SAUCE), EGGS OAXACA STYLE (REAR, RECIPE PAGE 53) AND MEXICAN-STYLE SCRAMBLED EGGS (FRONT, RECIPE PAGE 54)

RECADO ROJO

ACHIOTE PASTE

1 tablespoon *achiote* (annatto) seeds
½ teaspoon ground cumin
¼ teaspoon dried oregano
8 black peppercorns
½ teaspoon ground allspice
1 whole clove
¼ teaspoon ground *chile piquín*
½ teaspoon salt
2 cloves garlic
3 tablespoons bitter (Seville) orange juice or

2 tablespoons orange juice mixed with
1 tablespoon white vinegar

In a nut or coffee grinder, grind the *achiote* seeds, cumin, oregano, peppercorns, allspice, clove, *chile piquín* and salt.

Grind the garlic in a mortar or *molcajete,* add the ground spice mixture and stir in the orange juice to make a paste. Place the *achiote* paste in a small glass jar, cover and refrigerate until ready to use in *pollo en escabeche* (page 64).

Makes about ⅓ cup (3 oz/90 g)

HUEVOS RANCHEROS

HUEVOS RANCHEROS

RANCH-STYLE EGGS

*In preindustrial times, two breakfasts were served—
coffee and* pan dulce *in the early hours and a more
substantial protein-based meal called* almuerzo *at
midmorning. These popular ranch-style eggs were
commonly eaten for the late breakfast, but now you*
*find them on menus at all hours of the day, served
with* frijoles refritos *(page 96) and extra tortillas.*

¼ cup (2 fl oz/60 ml) oil
1 tablespoon finely chopped onion
½ clove garlic, finely chopped
¾ cup (6 oz/185 g) finely chopped tomato
1 *chile serrano*, finely chopped

⅛ teaspoon each salt and freshly ground
pepper
1 corn tortilla
2 eggs

▨ Heat 1 tablespoon of the oil in a small
saucepan, add the onion and garlic and sauté
until transparent. Add the tomato and cook
for 2 minutes. Add the *chile,* salt and pepper
and cook another 3 minutes. Correct the
seasonings.

▨ Heat the remaining oil in a skillet, add the
tortilla, fry for 30 seconds and drain. Pour
off most of the oil, add the eggs and fry until
set. Place the tortilla on a plate, top with
the fried eggs and cover with the sauce.
Serve hot.

Serves 1

OMELETTE CON QUESO Y SALSA DE POBLANO
CHEESE OMELET WITH POBLANO SAUCE

*The French-style omelet is popular in such weekend
getaway spots as Cuernavaca, near Mexico City.*

⅓ cup (3 oz/90 g) chopped *chile poblano*
⅓ cup (3 fl oz/80 ml) thick cream *(crème fraîche)*
salt
⅛ teaspoon freshly ground pepper
2 eggs
1 tablespoon butter
¼ cup (1 oz/30 g) grated *queso manchego*
(or Monterey Jack or medium-sharp
Cheddar cheese)

▨ In a blender, purée the *chile* with the cream.
Add salt to taste and heat the sauce in a small
pan over medium heat; set aside.

▨ Add ½ teaspoon salt and the pepper to the
eggs and beat lightly.

▨ Melt the butter in a small skillet. When it
is hot, add the eggs. When the edge of the
eggs can be lifted easily, place the cheese on
one side, roll up and cook until the cheese
begins to melt. If the egg starts to brown, lower
the heat. Place on a plate and cover with the
hot *chile* cream.

▨ *Note:* This recipe can easily be tripled or
quadrupled. The omelets can be made in
advance, covered with the *poblano* sauce and
baked at 375°F (190°C) for 10 minutes.

Serves 1–2

CHEESE OMELET WITH POBLANO SAUCE

MANCHAMANTELES (TOP) AND PISTACHIO MOLE (BOTTOM)

MANCHAMANTELES

SLOPPY CHICKEN

The name for this sprightly dish, one of the seven moles of Oaxaca, is a Spanish translation for "tablecloth stainer," a title that well describes what happens if you spill any of the chile ancho *sauce. Tortillas are essential to sop up the sauce and keep spilling to a minimum.*

5 *chiles anchos,* seeds and membranes
   removed
½ onion
3 cloves garlic
1 3-in (7.5-cm) stick cinnamon
4 whole cloves

4 black peppercorns
5 blanched almonds
½ teaspoon each dried oregano and thyme
3 tablespoons oil
3 large ripe tomatoes
1 chicken, about 3 lb (1.5 kg), cut into
   serving pieces
1½–2 cups (12–16 fl oz/375–500 ml) water
1 teaspoon salt
1 small sprig parsley
1 sweet potato, about 8 oz (250 g), peeled
   and cubed
1 tablespoon butter
2 cups (11 oz/345 g) sliced plantain or large
   firm banana
2 slices pineapple (10 oz/315 g), cubed

▓ Toast the *chiles* (see glossary) on a *comal* or iron skillet, then soak in hot water to cover for 20 minutes. Drain.

▓ Roast the onion, garlic, cinnamon, cloves, peppercorns, almonds, oregano and thyme (see glossary). Transfer to a blender, add the *chiles* and purée.

▓ Heat 1 tablespoon of the oil in a large saucepan. Add the purée and boil vigorously, stirring constantly, for 5 minutes.

▓ Roast the tomatoes (see glossary), peel and purée in a blender. Add to the *chile* purée, lower the heat and cook for 7 minutes, stirring constantly. Set aside.

▓ Heat the remaining 2 tablespoons oil in a large skillet, add the chicken and sauté until lightly browned. Add the water, salt and parsley. When the water comes to a boil, lower the heat and cook, covered, for 10 minutes. Add the *chile* sauce and continue cooking for 10 minutes. Add the sweet potato and cook an additional 10 minutes.

▓ Melt the butter in a small skillet, add the plantains and pineapple and sauté until lightly browned. Add to the chicken, correct the seasonings and cook, covered, over low heat for 15 minutes or until the chicken is tender.

Serves 6

Distrito Federal

MOLE DE PISTACHE
PISTACHIO MOLE

Martha Chapa puts together the unusual and delicate combination of pistachios and avocado leaves in this new version of mole.

8 chicken legs with thighs
3 cups (24 fl oz/750 ml) white wine
3 cups (24 fl oz/750 ml) water
2 onions, sliced
4 cloves garlic
4 avocado leaves, fresh or dried
salt
6 tablespoons (3 oz/90 g) butter
2 tablespoons oil
1 *chile poblano,* roasted (see glossary), peeled and membranes removed
10 oz (315 g) shelled pistachios, skins removed
freshly ground pepper

GARNISH
½ onion, sliced
1 tablespoon butter
fresh avocado leaves (optional)

▓ In a large covered saucepan over medium heat, simmer the chicken in the wine and water along with 1 onion and the garlic, avocado leaves and salt until tender, about 30 minutes. Drain the chicken, reserving the stock, and return to the saucepan.

▓ While the chicken is cooking, heat the butter and oil in a skillet. Add the *chile,* remaining onion and the pistachios and sauté until lightly browned. In a blender or food processor, grind this mixture with a little of the reserved stock, then simmer in a covered saucepan over very low heat for 30 minutes. Pour over the chicken and simmer, covered, for 5 minutes. Correct the seasonings.

▓ In a small skillet, sauté the onion in the butter for 5 minutes or until translucent. Garnish with the onions and fresh avocado leaves.

Serves 4–6

SALSA DE JITOMATE
TOMATO SAUCE

2½ lb (1.25 kg) tomatoes, peeled and cut
    into chunks
1 clove garlic
¼ onion
¼ teaspoon dried thyme
¼ teaspoon ground cumin
1 whole clove
¼ cup (2 fl oz/60 ml) water
1 tablespoon butter
1 teaspoon salt
¼ teaspoon freshly ground pepper

◙ In a blender, purée the tomatoes, garlic, onion, thyme, cumin, clove and water. Melt the butter in a small skillet, add the purée, salt and pepper and boil for 5 minutes. Lower the heat and cook, uncovered, for 10 minutes.
◙ Serve with *albondigón relleno de rajas* (page 74)

Makes 2½ cups (20 fl oz/750 ml)

Oaxaca

PIERNA DE CERDO ADOBADA
ROAST LEG OF PORK IN ADOBO SAUCE

This makes a festive buffet dish served with arroz a la Mexicana *(page 42) and* ensalada rosaura *(page 98). Any leftover pork is ideal as a meat filling for sandwiches.*

2 cups (16 fl oz/500 ml) freshly squeezed
    orange juice
8 *chiles pasillas*, seeds and membranes
    removed

6 *chiles anchos,* seeds and membranes removed
¼ onion
⅓ cup (3 fl oz/80 ml) cider vinegar
10 cloves garlic
1 teaspoon dried thyme
3 whole cloves
1 teaspoon ground cumin
1 tablespoon dried oregano
1 2-in (5-cm) stick cinnamon
3 whole allspice
2 tablespoons coarse salt
1 leg of pork, about 9 lb (4.5 kg)
2 tablespoons (1 oz/30 g) lard

◙ In a small saucepan, heat 1 cup (8 fl oz/250 ml) of the orange juice until warm. Toast the *chiles* (see glossary) on a *comal* or iron skillet, then let them soak in the orange juice for 20 minutes. Transfer the *chiles* and orange juice to a blender, add the onion and vinegar and purée. Set aside.
◙ In a mortar or a *molcajete,* grind the garlic, thyme, cloves, cumin, oregano, cinnamon, allspice and salt. Add the puréed *chiles* and stir well. Add enough orange juice to dilute the mixture until it has the consistency of yogurt.
◙ Use a fork to pierce the leg of pork all over. Transfer to a baking pan or dish, cover with the *chile*-orange sauce and refrigerate, covered, for at least 6 hours, preferably overnight. Turn occasionally.
◙ Two hours before roasting, remove the leg of pork from the refrigerator and smear the meat lightly with the lard. Let stand in the sauce at room temperature.
◙ Preheat the oven to 350°F (180°C). Cover the leg of pork with aluminum foil and roast for 2 hours, basting periodically with the pan

ROAST LEG OF PORK IN ADOBO SAUCE

juices. Turn the meat over, cover and roast about 1 more hour. When the meat can easily be pierced with a fork, in 2–3 hours, turn the oven temperature up to 450°F (230°C), uncover the meat and roast for 5–10 minutes or until browned, being careful not to let it burn. Let stand for 15 minutes before slicing.

If you wish, you can double the quantity of the sauce and serve the extra to accompany the sliced pork.

Serves 12–16

San Luis Potosí

ALBONDIGÓN RELLENO DE RAJAS
STUFFED MEAT LOAF

This special meat loaf was presented at a culinary festival of Mexican cooking in 1975. On slicing, the red and green strips of chile *make a colorful presentation.*

1 *bolillo* (hard bread roll), sliced and
   soaked in milk
1 clove garlic
¼ onion
1 teaspoon dried oregano
1 teaspoon ground cumin
3 whole cloves
1 teaspoon salt
½ teaspoon freshly ground pepper
2½ lb (1.25 kg) beef steak, ground (minced)
   twice
1 lb (500 g) lean pork, ground (minced)
   twice
3 eggs
1 tablespoon dry breadcrumbs
3 *chiles poblanos,* roasted (see glossary),
   membranes removed and cut into strips
1 jar (6½ oz/200 g) roasted red peppers,
   drained and cut into strips
8 oz (250 g) sliced bacon
salsa de jitomate (page 72)

❧ Preheat the oven to 350°F (180°C). Drain the *bollillo*, tear into small pieces and transfer to a large bowl. In a food processor or *molcajete,* grind the garlic, onion, oregano, cumin, cloves, salt and pepper. Transfer to the bowl and add the beef, pork, eggs and breadcrumbs. Use your hands to combine thoroughly.

❧ Transfer to a clean board and pat into a rectangle. Arrange the *chile* and pepper strips down the center. Roll up lengthwise to form a loaf, place in a baking pan, top with bacon strips and bake for 1 hour.
❧ Serve with *salsa de jitomate* (page 72).

Serves 6–8

Distrito Federal

ROPA VIEJA
SHREDDED BEEF WITH VEGETABLES

The literal name of this dish— "old clothes"— is very apt and descriptive, as it is a good way to use up leftover cooked beef. The traditional ropa vieja *is used as a filling for* tacos, *but this variation includes a vinaigrette and is served as a cold salad.*

1 lb (500 g) beef flank steak, cut into
   2–3 pieces
2 bay leaves
1 clove garlic
1 tablespoon salt
¼ onion
1 carrot
1 sprig parsley
½ onion, sliced and separated into rings
⅓ cup (3 fl oz/80 ml) olive oil
2 tablespoons red wine vinegar, or to taste
1 tablespoon dried oregano
¼ teaspoon freshly ground pepper
2 tomatoes, cut into chunks
1 head of lettuce, chopped
1 avocado, peeled and sliced
6 radishes, cut in half (optional)

SHREDDED BEEF WITH VEGETABLES (TOP) AND STUFFED MEAT LOAF (BOTTOM)

Place the beef, bay leaves, garlic, salt, onion quarter, carrot and parsley in a large heavy saucepan. Add water to cover, bring to a boil, lower the heat, then simmer, covered, until the beef is tender, about 1 hour. Let the meat cool in the stock, then drain and shred.

In a bowl, mix the beef, onion, oil, vinegar, oregano and pepper. Let stand for 30 minutes.

Ten minutes before serving, add the tomatoes and a handful of the lettuce and toss to mix. Arrange a bed of lettuce on a platter and place the meat mixture in the center. Arrange the avocado slices on top and garnish with radish halves if desired.

Serves 4

BEEF TIPS MEXICAN STYLE (TOP) AND TINGA POBLANA (BOTTOM)

Chihuahua
PUNTAS DE FILETE A LA MEXICANA
BEEF TIPS MEXICAN STYLE

The beef industry began in Mexico in 1530 with a group of colonists headed by Vasco de Quiroga. In the small restaurants of the north, where this dish is most often found, queso fundido con champiñones y rajas de poblano *(page 12) and* frijoles refritos *(page 96) might likely share the table along with floppy flour tortillas.*

2 lb (1 kg) beef filet (rib eye) tips, cut
   into strips
3 cloves garlic, crushed

½ teaspoon freshly ground pepper
¼ teaspoon ground cumin
2 teaspoons salt
2 tablespoons oil
1 cup (8 oz/250 g) finely chopped onion
2 cloves garlic, minced
2½ lb (1.25 kg) ripe tomatoes, peeled and
   finely chopped
6 *chiles serranos*, finely chopped

▓ Mix the beef tips with the crushed garlic cloves, pepper, cumin and 1 teaspoon of the salt. Cover and refrigerate for at least 2 hours, preferably overnight.

Heat the oil in a large skillet or Dutch oven, add the onion and sauté for 4 minutes or until transparent. Add the minced garlic and the beef tips, stirring over high heat until the beef is browned, about 7 minutes. Add the tomatoes, *chiles* and remaining teaspoon of salt. Cook, uncovered, over medium heat for 10 minutes or until the sauce thickens and the meat is tender.

Variation: Substitute 3 pickled *chiles chipotles* for the *chiles serranos.*

Serves 6

Puebla

TINGA POBLANA

SHREDDED PORK AND BEEF WITH CHIPOTLE AND TOMATES VERDES

Bunches of dried thyme, marjoram and oregano are sold as hierbas de olor *(scented herbs) in virtually every Mexican market. These spices add flavor to this smoky- and spicy-tasting meat stew from Puebla. It is also used as a topping for crispy* tostadas, *garnished with shredded lettuce and sliced avocado.*

8 oz (250 g) boneless lean pork, cut
   into chunks
1 lb (500 g) beef flank steak, cut
   into chunks
2 bay leaves
2 cloves garlic
salt
1 lb (500 g) *chorizo* or other spicy sausage
1 onion, coarsely chopped
1 clove garlic, minced

1½ lb (750 g) ripe tomatoes, peeled and
   coarsely chopped
8 oz (250 g) *tomates verdes,* husks removed
   and finely sliced
½ teaspoon dried oregano
1 small sprig marjoram
1 small sprig thyme
¼ teaspoon freshly ground pepper
¼ cup (2 fl oz/ 60 ml) pickled *chile chipotle* juice
3 pickled *chiles chipotles,* cut into strips

Place the meat in a large pot or Dutch oven and cover with cold water. Bring to a boil over high heat and skim the surface. Lower the heat and add the bay leaves, garlic cloves and 1 teaspoon salt. Cover and cook over low heat for 1 hour or until the meat is tender. Let cool in the stock, then drain, reserving the stock. Shred the meat and set aside.

Remove the casing from the *chorizo* and cut into large chunks. Place in a skillet and fry over medium heat until lightly browned and some of the fat has been rendered. Remove the *chorizo* and set aside. Add the onion and minced garlic to the skillet and sauté for 2 minutes. Add the tomatoes, *tomates verdes,* oregano, marjoram, thyme, pepper and 1 tablespoon salt. Simmer over low heat for 5 minutes, stirring occasionally. Add the *chipotle* juice and stir.

Add the shredded meat to the skillet, stir well and add 1 cup (8 fl oz/250 ml) of the reserved stock. Add the *chorizo,* cover and cook over low heat for 15 minutes. If the sauce is too thick, add more stock.

Serve very hot, garnished with *chile* strips.

Serves 6

Puebla

LOMO DE CERDO MECHADO CON CHILES CHIPOTLES Y CIRUELAS

PORK ROAST STUFFED WITH CHILES CHIPOTLES AND PRUNES

The cooks from Catalonia in northeastern Spain have always paired meat with fruit, especially pears and prunes, in dishes similar to this Mexican version, which adds the picante *flavor of* chile chipotle.

1 pork loin, about 2½ lb (1.25 kg)
6 oz (185 g) pitted prunes (cut in half if large)
4 pickled *chiles chipotles,* each cut into
  4 pieces
1 clove garlic, crushed
salt and freshly ground pepper
2 cups (16 fl oz/500 ml) freshly squeezed
  orange juice
3 tablespoons all-purpose (plain) flour
2 tablespoons oil
1 large onion, sliced

▨ With a knife, make regularly spaced slits on the sides and bottom of the pork loin. Place a prune in one, a *chile* in the next, continuing until you have used all the *chiles* and prunes. Place the pork in a dish and rub with the garlic, salt and pepper. Pour the orange juice over the pork, cover and refrigerate for at least 2 hours, preferably overnight.
▨ Preheat the oven to 350°F (180°C). Drain the meat, reserving the juice in which it marinated. Sprinkle lightly with the flour. Heat the oil in a large skillet, add the pork and brown lightly on all sides, about 8 minutes.
▨ Arrange a layer of onion over the bottom of a lightly greased baking pan. Place the pork loin on top.

▨ Add the orange juice marinade to the skillet in which the pork was browned and scrape the bottom of the pan. Strain this juice over the pork and sprinkle with salt. Cover with aluminum foil and bake for 40 minutes. Uncover the meat, turn it over and baste with the pan juices. Roast, uncovered, 30 minutes longer or until a meat thermometer registers 170°F (80°C).

Serves 6–8   *Photograph page 50*

Yucatán

COCHINITA PIBIL

PORK BAKED IN LEAVES

In the Mayan language, pibes *are stone-lined pits, and* pibil *refers to the technique of cooking underground, though nowadays the meat is often steamed in a sealed dish in the oven. The savory meat and red onion salsa are rolled into tortillas and served with black beans, downed with* horchata *or beer. Pig's ears and cheeks are an authentic and tasty addition and can be ordered from most butchers.*

8 oz (250 g) pig's ears (optional)
8 oz (250 g) pig's cheeks (optional)
3 lb (1.5 kg) boneless lean pork
3 oz (90 g) *achiote* paste (page 67)
½ cup (4 fl oz/125 ml) lime juice
1 cup (8 fl oz/250 ml) freshly squeezed
  orange juice
2 teaspoons salt
2 large banana leaves
½ cup (4 oz/125 g) lard, melted

ONION *SALSA*
2 cups (15 oz/470 g) chopped red onion

1 cup (8 fl oz/250 ml) freshly squeezed
   orange juice
1 cup (8 fl oz/250 ml) lime juice
1 teaspoon salt
6 *chiles manzanos* or *chiles habaneros*

Cut the meat into 2-in (5-cm) pieces and place in a glass or ceramic dish. Place the *achiote* paste in a small glass bowl and add the juices to dissolve it, using your fingers to help break it up. Add the salt. Pour this liquid over the pork, cover and marinate in the refrigerator for at least 3 hours, preferably overnight.

Preheat the oven to 325°F (165°C). Hold the banana leaves directly over the flame on the stove for a few minutes, until they soften. Line a rectangular baking dish with the leaves, placing one the long way and the other the short way, with their ends overlapping the sides of the dish. Place the pork and marinade on the leaves and baste with the lard. Fold the ends of the leaves over the pork, moistening slightly so they do not burn. Cover the dish with aluminum foil.

Bake for 2 hours. Remove from the oven and uncover the meat. It should be tender, almost falling apart; if it isn't, cover and return to the oven for another 30 minutes.

Four hours before serving, prepare the onion *salsa*. Place the onion in a bowl and add the juices and salt. Toast the whole *chiles* (see glossary) and add them to the onions.

Serve the pork hot and pass the onion *salsa* separately.

Serves 6–8

PORK BAKED IN LEAVES

PESCADOS Y MARISCOS

SMALL WONDER that seafood plays such a major role in Mexican cuisine when more than half of its states have shores on the Sea of Cortés, the Pacific Ocean, the Gulf of Mexico or the Caribbean Sea.

Early every morning in the white- and blue-tiled fish markets of port cities, blackboards list the day's catches and their going prices. In the many villages lining the coast, buyers choose their purchases from piles of fish lying in the bows of incoming fishing boats.

Seafood should be cooked quickly and simply. About as simple as you can get is *ceviche* (or *cebiche* or *seviche*), a spirit-reviving dish of bite-size pieces of raw fish cooked by the acidic juice of freshly squeezed lime rather than heat. Most authorities agree that *ceviche* was first seen in Mexico in the port city of Acapulco during the 1500s, although there is evidence that Peruvian vessels may have reached Mexico earlier, bringing with them the technique of cooking fish without fire.

Quickly sautéed *huachinango* (red snapper) or skewered *róbalo* (snook) grilled over white-hot coals may be served directly from the fire with just a squeeze of lime or flavored with garlic or *chile chipotle*. Shellfish is similarly prepared, and a platter of *camarones al mojo de ajo*

(garlic shrimp) is about as sensual a dish as has ever been devised.

A simple but unforgettable meal is a plate full of *acamayes* (freshwater crayfish), which are sold by the kilo and eaten by hand.

Shrimp and other seafood are often shredded and made into fillings for *tacos, tamales* or *empanadas*. In the Gulf ports of Tampico and Veracruz, unusual azure-colored crabs are stuffed with a mixture of crabmeat, capers, onions, tomatoes and *chiles serranos*.

Preserved seafood is also eaten throughout Mexico, especially at the time of major holidays. Lent, with its forty days of penitential fasting, brings pyramids of dried shrimp, or *camarón seco,* to the markets.

Dried salt cod, because of its "keeping" qualities, was brought by the Spanish to the New World, where it became a dietary standby for people living far from the shore. The cod is salted and dried until hard as a board, then soaked to soften the flesh and remove the salt before the fish can be combined with *chiles,* tomatoes and potatoes in the tasty stew traditionally served at Christmastime.

Fish or shellfish, fresh or dried, from fresh or salt water—all blend perfectly with the piquant flavors of Mexico.

AVOCADOS STUFFED WITH SCALLOPS (RECIPE PAGE 89)

TIRITAS DE PESCADO

MARINATED STRIPS OF FISH

This version of ceviche *is a specialty in the beachside restaurants of Zihuatanejo.*

1 lb (500 g) red snapper fillets
¾ cup (6 fl oz/180 ml) lime juice
3 *chiles serranos,* seeded and cut into thin strips
1 cup (8 oz/250 g) thinly sliced red onion
1 tablespoon salt
¼ teaspoon freshly ground pepper
1 tablespoon dried oregano

◼ Cut the fish into strips 2 in (5 cm) long and ¼ in (5 mm) wide. Place in a glass bowl and add the lime juice, *chiles,* onion, salt, pepper and oregano. Stir and marinate for 10 minutes. Drain off the excess lime juice and correct the seasonings.
◼ Serve cold or at room temperature.

Serves 6

CÓCTEL DE CAMARONES CON ADEREZO DE AGUACATE

SHRIMP COCKTAIL WITH AVOCADO DRESSING

Martha Chapa, a well-known painter and food writer, created this rich and unusual version of a shrimp cocktail.

1 lb (500 g) small shrimp (prawns)
2 cups (16 fl oz/500 ml) fish stock or bottled
   clam juice
1 bouquet garni

2 large avocados
½ onion
2 cloves garlic
1 cup (8 fl oz/250 ml) thick cream *(crème fraîche)*
1 *chile serrano,* seeds and membranes removed
2 tablespoons lime juice
½ cup (4 fl oz/125 ml) olive oil

MARINATED STRIPS OF FISH (LEFT) AND SHRIMP COCKTAIL WITH AVOCADO DRESSING (RIGHT)

In a covered saucepan, poach the shrimp in the stock with the bouquet garni. When the shrimp are cooked, in 2–3 minutes, drain, remove their shells and refrigerate.

While the shrimp cool, prepare the dressing by puréeing the remaining ingredients in a blender until a velvety texture is achieved.

Arrange alternate layers of shrimp and dressing in tall glasses. Refrigerate until ready to serve.

Variation: When this cocktail is enriched by the addition of poached lobster medallions, a truly extraordinary result is guaranteed.

Serves 4

FISH IN ALMOND SAUCE

Guerrero

PESCADO ALMENDRADO

FISH IN ALMOND SAUCE

This dish is well known among jet-setters, as it is based on a recipe from the famous Pipo's restaurant in Acapulco.

8 red snapper or sea bass fillets, about 4 oz
   (125 g) each
juice of 2 limes
1 teaspoon salt
¼ teaspoon freshly ground pepper
2 cups (16 fl oz/500 ml) thick cream *(crème fraîche)*
1 cup (5 oz/155 g) blanched almonds

2 tablespoons grated Parmesan cheese
¼ cup (2 oz/60 g) butter
1 cup (4 oz/125 g) grated *queso Chihuahua*
   (or Monterey Jack or medium-sharp
   Cheddar cheese)
8 small slices pickled *chiles jalapeños* (optional)
toasted slivered almonds, for garnish (optional)

▨ Marinate the fillets in the lime juice, salt and pepper for 1 hour in the refrigerator.
▨ Meanwhile, in a blender, purée the cream, almonds and Parmesan cheese. Set aside.
▨ Preheat the oven to 375°F (190°C). Melt the butter in a large skillet, add the fillets and

sauté lightly on both sides. Transfer to a greased baking dish and cover with the almond sauce. Sprinkle with the *queso Chihuahua* and bake for about 15 minutes or until the cheese melts.

▓ Garnish with the *chiles* and almonds.

Serves 8

Tamaulipas

COCO CON MARISCOS
SEAFOOD IN COCONUT SHELLS

Seafood stews are popular all along the Gulf coast, but this one from Tampico is unusual in that it is served in a hollowed coconut. Local cooks open coconuts with a machete, but a small saw works just as well. The shellfish can vary depending on what is available.

6 coconuts
2 lb (1 kg) octopus, cleaned
2 cups (16 fl oz/500 ml) water
2 cloves garlic
1 lb (500 g) medium shrimp (prawns)
20 clams in their shells
6 tablespoons (3 fl oz/90 ml) olive oil
1¾ cups (14 oz/440 g) chopped onion
1 tablespoon minced garlic
2½ lb (1.25 kg) tomatoes, peeled and chopped (5 cups)
1 teaspoon salt
8 oz (250 g) shucked (opened) scallops
1 cup (1½ oz/45 g) chopped parsley
10 oz (315 g) shucked (opened) small oysters
6 tablespoons (1½ oz/45 g) dry breadcrumbs
2 tablespoons (1 oz/30 g) butter, melted

▓ With a sharp heavy cleaver, cut off the tops of the coconuts. Pour out and save a total of

2 cups (16 fl oz/ 500 ml) coconut milk (coconut water) and set aside.

▓ Cook the octopus in a pressure cooker with ½ cup (4 fl oz/125 ml) of the water for 10 minutes or until tender. (Or place in a saucepan with 6 cups (48 fl oz/1.5 l) water, bring to a boil, cover and simmer for 45–60 minutes.) Drain, then scrape the octopus with a spoon to remove the suckers and cut into 1-in (2.5-cm) pieces. Set aside.

▓ Meanwhile, place 1 cup (8 fl oz/250 ml) of the water and the cloves of garlic in a saucepan, bring the water to a boil and add the shrimp. Cover and cook until the shrimp turn pink, about 4 minutes. Drain, reserving the cooking stock. Shell the shrimp and devein if needed.

▓ Rinse the clams and steam in the remaining ½ cup (4 fl oz/125 ml) water in a covered saucepan until they open. Drain, reserving all the liquid. Remove the clams from their shells and set aside.

▓ Preheat the oven to 375°F (190°C). Heat the oil in a large saucepan, add the onion and minced garlic and sauté until transparent. Add the tomatoes and salt and cook for 5 minutes. Add the coconut milk and reserved stock from the shrimp and clams. Bring to a boil and add the octopus, shrimp, clams, scallops and parsley. Cook, covered, for 5 minutes and correct the seasonings. Add the oysters and cook for 2 minutes.

▓ To serve, divide the seafood "soup" among the 6 coconut shells. Sprinkle with the breadcrumbs, drizzle with the butter and bake for 7 minutes.

Serves 6   *Photograph page 6*

Sinaloa

HUACHINANGO A LA NARANJA
RED SNAPPER WITH ORANGE SAUCE

The magnificent true red snapper is a Gulf coast fish, but other species abound all along Mexico's Pacific coast and are prepared in myriad ways. This unusual version has an orange sauce that gives the fish a tangy flavor. A slice of olive can be used to replace the eye if the appearance is a bother.

1 red snapper, about 4 lb (2 kg), cleaned
juice of 1 lime
2 cloves garlic, crushed
2 teaspoons salt
½ teaspoon freshly ground pepper
2 cups (16 fl oz/500 ml) orange juice
⅓ cup (3 oz/90 g) grated onion
1 cup (8 fl oz/250 ml) thick cream *(crème fraîche)*
1 orange, sliced

▩ Rub the fish with the lime juice and crushed garlic. Season with the salt and pepper and let stand for 1 hour.
▩ Preheat the oven to 375°F (190°C). Place the fish in a greased baking dish and cover with the orange juice. Sprinkle with the grated onion.
▩ Bake, uncovered, basting frequently with the pan juices, for 35 minutes or until the fish flakes easily when it is pierced with a fork.
▩ Remove the fish from the oven and cover it with the cream. Garnish with orange slices and serve.

Serves 6

Guerrero

HUACHINANGO AL PEREJIL
RED SNAPPER WITH PARSLEY CREAM

Parsley, preferably the flat-leafed Italian variety, is the flavoring for this sauce, accenting the fresh, light taste of the fish. If whole red snapper is not available, any fish with firm white flesh can be substituted.

1 red snapper, about 3 lb (1.5 kg), cleaned, with head and tail left on
2 tablespoons lime juice
1 clove garlic, finely chopped
salt and freshly ground pepper
2 cups (16 fl oz/500 ml) light (single) cream or half & half (half milk and half cream)
1 cup (1½ oz/45 g) chopped fresh parsley

▩ Preheat the oven to 325°F (165°C). Rinse the fish and pat dry.
▩ Combine the lime juice, garlic and salt and pepper to taste. Rub the entire fish, inside and out, with this mixture and let it marinate for 20 minutes.
▩ Meanwhile, purée the cream and parsley in a blender until smooth. Add salt and pepper to taste.
▩ Place the fish in a greased baking dish. Cover with the parsley cream and bake for about 30 minutes or until the fish is cooked (the time will vary depending on the thickness of the fish).

Serves 4

INGREDIENTS FOR RED SNAPPER WITH ORANGE SAUCE (TOP), FISH VERACRUZ STYLE (CENTER, RECIPE PAGE 91) AND RED SNAPPER WITH PARSLEY CREAM (BOTTOM)

SNOOK WITH PARSLEY AND CRAYFISH (LEFT) AND CRAB AND CACTUS PADDLE COCKTAIL (RIGHT)

Colima

ROBALO AL PEREJIL CON LANGOSTINOS

SNOOK WITH PARSLEY AND CRAYFISH

Langostinos *are freshwater crustaceans, similar to crayfish, that grow especially well in the estuaries of Colima, where they are also called* chacales. *On the Gulf coast, where they may reach ten inches in size, they are called* acamayas.

8 cloves garlic, crushed
2 teaspoons salt
2 tablespoons lime juice

6 fillets of snook, sea bass or other
    firm-fleshed fish, about 5 oz (155 g) each
1 lb (500 g) crayfish or large shrimp
    (or marron, scampi or Balmain bugs)
⅓ cup (3 fl oz/80 ml) olive oil
1 cup (8 oz/250 g) finely chopped onion
2 tablespoons chopped garlic
1⅓ cups (2 oz/60 g) finely chopped parsley
2–3 *chiles serranos* (optional)
2 cups (16 fl oz/500 ml) white wine
1 cup (8 fl oz/250 ml) fish stock or bottled
    clam juice
1 teaspoon salt

Combine the crushed garlic, salt and lime juice in a glass dish, add the fillets and the crayfish and marinate, refrigerated, for at least 2 hours, turning occasionally.

Heat the oil in a small *paella* pan or a *cazuela*. Add the onion and chopped garlic and sauté for 4 minutes or until transparent. Add the parsley and *chiles* and stir for 2 minutes. Add the wine, fish stock and salt. When the mixture comes to a boil, lower the heat and add the crayfish. Cover and cook for 5 minutes. Add the fish and cook for 7 minutes or until done. Serve at once.

If you want a thicker sauce, dust the fillets lightly with flour.

Serves 6

Baja California Norte

CALLO DE HACHA CON AGUACATE
AVOCADOS STUFFED WITH SCALLOPS

It is more customary to find avocados stuffed with tiny shrimp than with scallops, but this combination is, if anything, even more tasty. The original recipe uses chocolata *scallops, a dark-shelled species found mostly around the Sea of Cortez, but small bay scallops may be substituted.*

12 oz (375 g) shucked (opened) scallops
⅓ cup (3 fl oz/80 ml) fresh lime juice
1 tablespoon minced fresh oregano
1 tablespoon minced fresh *cilantro* (coriander)
⅔ cup (5 fl oz/160 ml) olive oil
salt and freshly ground pepper
3 large avocados, ripe but slightly firm
minced *chile serrano* (optional)

Place the scallops in a bowl and add the lime juice, oregano, *cilantro* and oil. Season with salt and pepper and let stand for 15–20 minutes or until opaque.

Cut each avocado in half, remove the pit and spoon out balls of the pulp, reserving the shells. Mix the avocado balls with the scallops and spoon into the avocado shells. If you wish, sprinkle minced *chile serrano* on top.

Serves 6   *Photograph page 80*

Oaxaca

SALPICÓN DE JAIBA Y NOPALITOS
CRAB AND CACTUS PADDLE COCKTAIL

A Spanish dictionary will translate salpicón *as "medley," "splashing" or even "salmagundi," which all comes down to any number of mixtures of shredded meat and fish served in different parts of Mexico. This tasty dish from Martha Chapa is easy to prepare on hot days.*

1 cup (8 fl oz/250 ml) tomato sauce (puréed tomatoes)
8 oz (250 g) tomatoes, peeled and diced
½ teaspoon Worcestershire sauce
½ teaspoon Tabasco sauce
3 paddles of nopal cactus (8 oz/250 g), cooked and diced (see glossary)
10 oz (315 g) cooked crabmeat, flaked
3 tablespoons finely chopped *cilantro* (coriander)

Combine all the ingredients, mix well and chill for several hours. Serve in tall glasses.

Serves 4–6

GARLIC SHRIMP

CAMARONES AL MOJO DE AJO
GARLIC SHRIMP

Garlic is seldom used in prodigious amounts in Mexican cooking, but in this popular shrimp dish *it provides a perfect balance of flavors. Rice is a natural accompaniment.*

36 medium shrimp (prawns) in their shells
15 cloves garlic, 3 whole, 12 minced
¾ teaspoon salt

¾ teaspoon freshly ground pepper
¾ teaspoon white vinegar
3 tablespoons olive oil
5 tablespoons (2½ oz/80 g) butter
3 tablespoons lime juice

▨ From the underside, split the shrimp down the middle without separating them completely. Remove the dark vein if apparent.
▨ In a blender, purée the whole garlic cloves, salt, pepper and vinegar. Marinate the shrimp in this mixture for 30 minutes.
▨ Heat the oil and butter in a skillet. Add the minced garlic and sauté until golden brown, about 3 minutes. Add the shrimp with the shell sides up. Lower the heat, cover and cook for 2–3 minutes or until the shrimp are opaque. Sprinkle with the lime juice and remove from the heat.

Serves 6

Veracruz

PESCADO A LA VERACRUZANA
FISH VERACRUZ STYLE

This famous fish dish combines chiles *and tomatoes from the New World with the very Spanish addition of capers and olives. It is traditionally served with a scoop of white rice.*

---

1 tablespoon oil
4 cloves garlic, chopped
½ cup (4 oz/125 g) finely chopped onion
2 lb (1 kg) tomatoes, peeled and finely chopped
1 green bell pepper (capsicum), cut into strips
1 teaspoon salt

½ teaspoon freshly ground pepper
2 bay leaves
1 teaspoon dried oregano
½ cup (2½ oz/75 g) chopped green olives
¼ cup (2 oz/60 g) capers
6 fillets of sea bass or other firm-fleshed fish, about 4 oz (125 g) each
2 tablespoons (1 oz/30 g) butter
6 canned *chiles güeros* or *jalapeños,* for garnish

▨ Heat the oil in a large saucepan, add the garlic and onion and sauté for 3 minutes. Add the tomatoes and bring to a boil. Add the bell pepper and stir for 2 minutes. Add the salt, pepper, bay leaves and oregano. When the mixture returns to a boil, cover and cook over low heat for 8 minutes. Add the olives and capers and cook another 5 minutes. Correct the seasonings and remove from heat.
▨ Twenty minutes before serving, preheat the oven to 375°F (190°C). Rinse the fillets, pat dry and sprinkle lightly with salt and pepper. Melt the butter in a large skillet, add the fillets and brown lightly on both sides. Transfer to a greased baking dish and cover with the sauce. Cover the dish with aluminum foil and bake for 10–15 minutes. Garnish each fillet with a *chile* before serving.
▨ *Note:* You can use a whole fish if you prefer, but you will need to increase the baking time.

Serves 6   *Photograph page 87*

VERDURAS, ENSALADAS, FRIJOLES Y SALSAS

TOTTERING MOUNDS of maize, baskets of beans—red, black, white, multicolored, speckled and striped—cacao, peppers, onions, a thousand kinds of green stuff, fruits, sweet potatoes and squashes greeted Hernán Cortés when he first reached the great marketplace of Tlatelolco at the center of the Aztec empire.

The same vegetables are prized today. They appear in just about every course put on the table—even dessert, which may be a dish of mashed and flavored sweet potato.

Squash has always played an important role in the Mexican diet. The *pepitas* (dried seeds) are eaten plain as snacks, or ground for flavoring and thickening the many varieties of *pipianes*. Squash flowers have long been considered a delicacy, and the delicate young squash vines are made into a popular soup. Another member of this family is the pear-shaped *chayote,* which alone does not have a distinctive flavor or texture; but with a little garlic or tomato or *chile,* becomes a very interesting vegetable. *Nopales* (cactus paddles), minus their prickles, are used in salads, *tacos* and scrambled eggs.

Cilantro (coriander), also called Chinese parsley because of its use in many Oriental cuisines, has a unique pungent flavor that complements spicy dishes. In the southern states of Mexico, a pot of black beans without the herb *epazote* is simply incomplete, and the musky *hierba santa* seasons *tamales,* chicken and fish. This giant plant has velvety leaves that impart a sarsaparilla flavor to food.

The luscious, sensual spiciness of *chiles* is the seasoning most identified with Mexican cooking. The same *chile* may be known by different names in Mexico, depending on whether it is fresh or dried or depending on the region in which it is grown.

Tomatoes and *chiles,* onions and garlic are the basis for the *salsas* that accompany virtually every Mexican meal—every plate of eggs, every bowl of soup or piece of meat.

Salsas are also made from the wonderful but confusing *tomate verde* (green tomato), which is not a true tomato, though it is a member of the same nightshade family. This small lime-green fruit is available canned in specialty food stores, and many supermarkets and greengrocers now carry the fresh *tomate verde* under the name *tomatillo.*

Frijoles (beans) are eaten by all classes of people and in all parts of Mexico and the world. While a few—the fava, chickpea and soybean—originated in the Old World, most of the protein-rich legumes that we eat today have long been a part of the Mexican diet.

CHAYOTE SALAD (LEFT, RECIPE PAGE 99) AND GREEN BEANS WITH ONION AND TOMATO (RIGHT, RECIPE PAGE 100)

SALSA DE MOLCAJETE

MOLCAJETE SAUCE

While most table salsas are either fresh or cooked, in this version the flavor of the chiles and tomatoes is intensified by roasting. Some salsas can be made in a blender, but the texture of this one is much better when made in the traditional molcajete, as it is important that it be chunky, not smooth. This salsa complements any of the masa antojitos in Chapter 1.

5 *chiles serranos*
2 ripe tomatoes
1 clove garlic
1 teaspoon salt

▨ On a *comal* or iron skillet, roast the *chiles* and tomatoes (see glossary) for 8 minutes or until they are soft. Peel off and discard the burned skin from the tomatoes. In a mortar or *molcajete*, grind the *chiles* and garlic. When they are roughly chopped, add the tomatoes and continue grinding. Add the salt. Serve in the *molcajete* or a small bowl.

Makes 1½ cups (12 fl oz/375 ml)

Michoacán

SALSA DE TOMATE VERDE CON AGUACATE

TOMATE VERDE SAUCE WITH AVOCADO

Avocado has been added to this green table salsa, which makes it a richer condiment. The rest of the salsa can be made in advance, refrigerated and combined with avocado before serving.

5 *chiles serranos*
10 oz (315 g) *tomates verdes,* husks removed
1 clove garlic
1 tablespoon vinegar from pickled *chiles*
1 pickled *chile serrano,* seeds removed
1 teaspoon salt
½ cup (¾ oz/20 g) coarsely chopped *cilantro* (coriander)
1 avocado, peeled, pitted and cubed
⅓ cup (3 oz/90 g) finely chopped onion

▨ Place the fresh *chiles* in a large saucepan of boiling water. After 5 minutes, add the *tomates verdes.* After about 3 minutes, remove the *chiles* and *tomates verdes* and drain.
▨ Purée the *chiles, tomates verdes,* garlic, vinegar and pickled *chile* in a blender. Add the salt and *cilantro* and blend for 2 short cycles.
▨ In a bowl, combine the purée, avocado and onion. Correct the seasonings.

Makes about 1½ cups (12 fl oz/375 ml)

Guerrero

SALSA COSTEÑA

CHILE COSTEÑO SAUCE

This table salsa is made with the searing-hot chile costeño, which is difficult to find outside the Pacific coast region of Mexico. The equally hot but shorter and wider dried chile de árbol can be substituted. Serve this sauce with fish, meat or chicken.

6 *chiles costeños*
8 *tomates verdes,* about ½ lb (250 g), husks removed
1 clove garlic

TOP TO BOTTOM: CHILE COSTEÑO SAUCE, MOLCAJETE SAUCE, TOMATE VERDE SAUCE WITH AVOCADO

½ cup (4 oz/125 g) chopped onion
⅓ cup (½ oz/15 g) chopped *cilantro*
   (coriander)
½ teaspoon salt

▨ Toast the *chiles* on a *comal* or iron skillet (see glossary). They should turn dark but not be allowed to burn.

▨ In a saucepan, cook the *tomates verdes* in boiling salted water for 5 minutes. Drain.

▨ In a blender, purée the *chiles* with the *tomates verdes* and garlic. Do not strain. Transfer to a sauce dish, add the onion, *cilantro* and salt and stir. Correct the seasonings.

Makes 1 cup (8 fl oz/250 ml)

REFRIED BEANS

FRIJOLES REFRITOS
REFRIED BEANS

Here is one dish where using a flavorful homemade lard definitely makes a difference. Canned beans, in a pinch, can be substituted for the frijoles de la olla, *using approximately 1 cup water (in place of the bean liquid) to 3 cups beans. Don't think that* refritos *means to fry twice; it simply means "well fried"—until all the liquid is gone.*

½ cup (4 oz/125 g) lard or oil
½ onion, cut into chunks
4 cups (32 fl oz/1 l) *frijoles de la olla*
  (recipe follows) with their liquid
crumbled *queso fresco* (or feta cheese) (optional)
fried tortilla strips★ (optional)

Melt the lard in a large skillet, add the onion and sauté, stirring frequently, for 5 minutes or until golden and soft. Remove and discard onion. Add half of the beans with their liquid and mash in the skillet with a potato masher. Gradually add the remaining beans and liquid and continue mashing to make a coarse purée. Stir and cook over medium-high heat until the purée begins to dry out.

Transfer to a warm platter, sprinkle with cheese and garnish with tortilla strips.

Variation: If you like the taste of onion, you can use finely chopped onion, in which case do not discard.

★Cut 4 day-old corn tortillas in half, then cut into ½-in (1.5-cm) strips. Heat ½ in (1 cm) oil in a small skillet and, when hot, add the tortilla strips a few at a time and fry, turning at least once, for about 3 minutes or until golden brown. Remove from the oil with a slotted spatula and drain on absorbent paper. (If using fresh tortillas, dry first in a preheated 250°F/120°C oven for an hour.)

Serves 6

Tabasco

FRIJOLES DE LA OLLA
POT BEANS

Since, as it is said in Mexico, "not even mice will eat raw beans," the simmering olla *(clay pot) of beans is a constant in most kitchens. In modern Mexican homes, however, beans are often cooked in a pressure cooker, but they always seem to taste better made the traditional way.*

2 cups (12 oz/375 g) dried black, pinto or
  pink beans

10 cups (80 fl oz/2.5 l) water
⅓ onion
3 tablespoons (1½ oz/50 g) lard or bacon drippings
1 sprig *epazote*
2 teaspoons salt
3 *chiles serranos*

Rinse the beans, cover with room-temperature water and let soak for at least 3 hours. Discard any beans that float, then drain.

Place the beans in a large pot or Dutch oven and add the water, onion and lard. Cook, covered, over medium heat for 1½–2 hours or until tender. Make sure that there is always enough water to cover the beans; add more *hot* water if needed (be sure it is hot). When the beans are tender, uncover, add the *epazote,* salt and *chiles* and cook, uncovered, for 20 minutes. Correct the seasonings.

Serves 6

SALSA MEXICANA
MEXICAN SAUCE

If the sweet field-ripened tomato is used to make this classic condiment, which is served in every Mexican restaurant, it is the perfect complement to antojitos. Notice that the ingredients for this salsa should be finely chopped and not put in a blender.

3 ripe tomatoes, chopped
½ cup (4 oz/125 g) chopped onion
4–6 *chiles serranos,* chopped
½ cup (¾ oz/20 g) chopped *cilantro* (coriander)
2 teaspoons salt
2 teaspoons lime juice

Combine all the ingredients in a sauce dish. Stir well and correct the seasonings. This *salsa* is best if made 1 hour in advance so the flavors will blend.

Makes about 1½ cups (12 fl oz/375 ml)

MEXICAN SAUCE

ROSAURA SALAD

Distrito Federal

ENSALADA ROSAURA

ROSAURA SALAD

María Dolores Torres Yzábal won an award for this surprising salad at a Christmas food festival held at the Museum of Popular Cultures in Mexico City. Among its unusual ingredients is acitrón, *a candied cactus fruit native to the Baja Californias used mainly in* picadillos *(meat fillings) and Christmas breads.*

1 lb (500 g) red cabbage, thinly sliced
2 small raw beets, peeled and shredded

8 oz (250 g) spinach, thinly sliced
1 *jícama* (yam bean), about 10 oz/315 g, peeled and cut into sticks
½ onion, thinly sliced
3½ oz (100 g) *acitrón* (candied cactus), diced (if unavailable, use candied pineapple)
1 cup (3 oz/90 g) croutons
½ cup (2 oz/60 g) amaranth seeds or toasted sesame seeds

VINAIGRETTE
1½ teaspoons soy sauce
½ cup (4 fl oz/125 ml) corn oil
2 tablespoons cider vinegar

1 teaspoon (or to taste) chicken bouillon
   granules
1 teaspoon dried tarragon
½ teaspoon dried oregano
½ teaspoon *fines herbes*

AVOCADO DRESSING
1 cup (8 fl oz/250 ml) milk
1 clove garlic
1 tablespoon lime juice
1 cup (8 fl oz/250 ml) cream (any kind)
2 avocados
salt
1 tablespoon finely chopped chives

▦ Fifteen minutes before serving, combine the cabbage, beets, spinach, *jícama,* onion and *acitrón* in a salad bowl.

▦ To prepare the vinaigrette, mix all the ingredients together. (The vinaigrette can be made 6 hours in advance.)

▦ To prepare the avocado dressing, purée the milk and garlic in a blender. Add the lime juice, cream, avocados and salt to taste and blend until smooth. Pour into a small bowl and stir in the chives. (This dressing can be made half an hour in advance.)

▦ Add the vinaigrette to the salad and mix well. Sprinkle the croutons on top.

▦ Place the avocado dressing on one side of the salad bowl and a bowl of the amaranth or sesame seeds on the other. Each person takes a serving of the salad, adding the avocado dressing and a few of the seeds to taste.

Serves 12

Morelos

ENSALADA DE CHAYOTES
CHAYOTE SALAD

This simple salad makes use of the versatile chayote, *the fresher the better. In some rural areas, the* campesinos *(peasants) fry the leaves of the* chayote *plant as a tasty filling for* quesadillas.

---

2 lb (1 kg) *chayotes* (vegetable pears/chokos)
salt
6 tablespoons (3 fl oz/90 ml) oil
3 tablespoons red wine vinegar
½ teaspoon salt
¼ teaspoon freshly ground pepper
1 teaspoon dried oregano
½ red onion, thinly sliced and separated
   into rings

▦ Place the *chayotes,* unpeeled, in a large saucepan. Cover with water, add a pinch of salt and cook, covered, for 30–40 minutes or until they can easily be pierced with a fork.

▦ Drain and let cool for 5 minutes. Peel the *chayotes,* cut in half, then cut each half into 3 or 4 strips. Chill.

▦ Combine the oil, vinegar, salt, pepper and oregano. Stir well and correct the seasonings.

▦ Before serving, mix the *chayotes* with the dressing, top with the onion and sprinkle with more oregano if desired. Let stand for 5 minutes before serving.

Serves 6   *Photograph page 92*

Guerrero

PAPITAS DE CAMBRAY AL AJO
NEW POTATOES WITH GARLIC

In the markets throughout Mexico, it is a common sight to see pyramids of very tiny potatoes arranged on mats on the ground. This dish can accompany grilled meats; it also makes a popular party appetizer.

2 lb (1 kg) very small new potatoes, unpeeled
½ cup (4 oz/125 ml) butter
1 tablespoon oil
8 cloves garlic, minced (about 2 tablespoons)
1 tablespoon salt
1 teaspoon freshly ground pepper
1½ tablespoons lemon juice (optional)
½ teaspoon Tabasco sauce

☒ Cook the potatoes in boiling salted water until tender, 20–25 minutes. Drain and set aside.
☒ In a large saucepan, heat the butter and oil. Add the potatoes and sauté for 8–10 minutes. Add the garlic, salt, pepper, lemon juice and

NEW POTATOES WITH GARLIC

Tabasco sauce, lower the heat and cook for 3–4 minutes or until the garlic turns a golden color; be careful not to burn the garlic.

Serves 6

Guanajuato

EJOTES CON CEBOLLA Y JITOMATE
GREEN BEANS WITH ONION AND TOMATO

In the large haciendas of Guanajuato, cooked fresh vegetables were often prepared as side dishes, served lightly chilled or at room temperature.

2 lb (1 kg) green beans, cut into 1½-in (4-cm) lengths
2 cloves garlic
3 tablespoons red wine vinegar or to taste
1 small sprig thyme or 1 teaspoon dried thyme
½ teaspoon salt
¼ teaspoon freshly ground pepper
½ cup (4 fl oz/125 ml) olive oil
1 large tomato, chopped
¼ cup (2 oz/60 g) chopped onion
1 tablespoon dried oregano

☒ In a large saucepan, boil the beans in salted water for 8–10 minutes or until crisp-tender. Drain, then soak in ice water for 10 minutes. Drain, pat dry and set aside.
☒ Purée the garlic, vinegar, thyme, salt and pepper in a blender. With the motor running, add the oil in a thin stream.
☒ About 20 minutes before serving, combine the beans, tomato and onion. Add the vinaigrette and sprinkle with the oregano.

Serves 6   *Photograph page 92*

PICKLED CHILES AND VEGETABLES

CHILES Y VERDURAS EN ESCABECHE

PICKLED CHILES AND VEGETABLES

Attractive glass jars of pickled vegetables are displayed throughout central Mexico, and their enticing contents are used to accompany almost any main dish. They will last for several months in the refrigerator.

½ cup (4 fl oz/125 ml) oil
5 cloves garlic
4 carrots, sliced
8 oz (250 g) *chiles jalapeños,* cut in half, seeds and membranes removed
30 small white onions
3 small zucchini (courgettes), sliced
8 oz (250 g) small mushrooms
1 sprig thyme
1 sprig marjoram
5 bay leaves
2 teaspoons salt
¼ teaspoon freshly ground pepper
2 teaspoon dried oregano
2 cups (16 fl oz/500 ml) white vinegar
¾ cup (6 fl oz/180 ml) water

▦ In a large skillet, heat the oil, add the garlic and carrots and sauté for 2 minutes. Add the *chiles,* onions, zucchini and mushrooms and sauté 3 more minutes. Add the thyme, marjoram, bay leaves, salt, pepper and oregano and stir well. Add the vinegar and water, bring to a boil, lower the heat and simmer, covered, for 7 minutes. Remove from the heat and let stand, covered, for 15 minutes. ▦ Transfer to a heatproof bowl and let cool. Marinate for at least 12 hours before serving.

Serves 6

CHILES IN WALNUT SAUCE

Puebla

CHILES EN NOGADA
CHILES IN WALNUT SAUCE

This dish, resplendent with the red, white and green colors of the Mexican flag, was created by the imaginative Augustine nuns of Puebla for a visit by Mexico's very own emperor, Don Augustín de Iturbide, who, after the War of Independence, lasted a mere eleven months in office. It is featured as a main dish during August and September, when the new crop of walnuts is available. Although this dish appears complicated, the sauce and filling are best prepared the day before, and the chiles *can be stuffed several hours in advance.*

12 *chiles poblanos*
2 tablespoons salt
1 tablespoon white vinegar
5 eggs, separated
½ cup (2 oz/60 g) all-purpose (plain) flour
oil for frying
seeds of 1 pomegranate
sprigs of parsley, for garnish

NUT SAUCE
30 walnuts in their shells or 1 cup
    (3 oz/90 g) walnut halves
1½ cups (12 fl oz/375 ml) milk
1 cup (8 fl oz/250 ml) thick cream
    (*crème fraîche*)
6 oz (185 g) *queso fresco* (or feta cheese)
2–3 tablespoons sugar
pinch salt

FILLING
1 lb (500 g) pork loin
4 cups (32 fl oz/1 l) water
¼ onion, in a chunk
5 cloves garlic, 3 whole, 2 chopped
1 sprig parsley
1 tablespoon salt
⅓ cup (3 fl oz/80 ml) oil
¾ cup (6 oz/185 g) finely chopped onion
2 cups (1 lb/500 g) peeled and finely chopped
    tomatoes
4 tablespoons minced parsley
1 apple, peeled and chopped (about 1 cup)
1 large pear, peeled and chopped (about ¾ cup)
1 peach, peeled and chopped (about ½ cup)
1 plantain or large firm banana, peeled and
    chopped (about ¾ cup)
⅓ cup (2 oz/60 g) raisins
⅓ cup (2 oz/60 g) chopped blanched almonds

To prepare the nut sauce, shell the walnuts, place in a heatproof bowl, cover with boiling water and let soak for 5 minutes. Drain, then peel the thin tan skin from the nuts. Place the nuts in a small bowl, cover with 1 cup (8 fl oz/ 250 ml) of the milk and let soak for 12 hours.

Drain the walnuts, discarding the milk. (If packaged nuts are used, reserve ½ cup/4 fl oz/ 125 ml of the soaking milk for use in puréeing the nuts.) Transfer the walnuts to a blender and purée with the cream, the remaining ½ cup (4 fl oz/125 ml) milk and the *queso fresco,* sugar and salt. Refrigerate.

To prepare the filling, place the pork, water, onion quarter, 3 garlic cloves, parsley and half of the salt in a large saucepan. As soon as the water comes to a boil, cover and cook over medium heat for 40–60 minutes or until the pork is tender. Drain, reserving ½ cup (4 fl oz/125 ml) of the cooking stock. Let the pork cool briefly, then chop finely and set aside.

Heat the oil in a large skillet or saucepan. Add the chopped onion and garlic and sauté for 4 minutes or until transparent. Add the tomatoes and minced parsley and cook for 5 minutes, stirring constantly. Mix in the remaining salt and the apple, pear, peach, plantain, raisins and almonds and cook over medium heat for 4 minutes. Add the pork and the reserved stock. Correct the seasonings and cook, uncovered, over low heat for 7–10 minutes or until the fruit is cooked and the mixture has thickened. Set aside.

Roast and peel the *chiles* (see glossary). Make a lengthwise slit in each one, being careful not to break it, and remove the seeds and membranes. Soak the *chiles* in water to cover with the salt and vinegar for 20–60 minutes, depending on how "hot" they are.

Rinse the *chiles,* drain well and pat dry with paper towels. Use a spoon to place some of the meat mixture inside each *chile,* being careful not to overstuff or the filling will spill out when the *chile* is cooked. Set aside.

Beat the egg whites until they form stiff peaks, then stir in the yolks one at a time. Spread the flour on a plate, turn each *chile* in it to coat lightly, then dip into the beaten eggs, so that the *chile* is completely coated.

Heat ½ in (1 cm) oil in a skillet. When hot, add the *chiles* one or two at a time and fry on each side until lightly browned. Drain on absorbent paper. The *chiles* can be served cold or at room temperature. Arrange them on a platter, cover with the nut sauce and sprinkle with the pomegranate seeds. Garnish with sprigs of parsley.

Variations: There are as many minor variations of this recipe as there are people who prepare it. Some cooks add chopped citron, cinnamon and black pepper to the chopped meat mixture and a little sweet sherry or white wine to the nut sauce. Some use coarsely ground pork instead of cooked and chopped pork loin. The major difference is whether the *chiles* are covered with batter or not. Traditional recipes call for coating the *chiles,* but you may leave them uncoated, according to your taste and the amount of time you have to prepare them.

Serves 12

Puebla

CHILES RELLENOS DE QUESO
CHILES STUFFED WITH CHEESE

It is said that Emperor Maximilian liked a similar version of these cheese-stuffed chiles, only prepared with jocoque, *a rich, very thick soured cream.*

6 *chiles poblanos*
salt
2 teaspoons white vinegar
3 large ripe tomatoes
¼ small onion
1 clove garlic
1 tablespoon oil
2 bay leaves

CHILES STUFFED WITH CHEESE

½ teaspoon freshly ground pepper
3 cups (12 oz/375 g) grated *queso Chihuahua* (or Monterey Jack or medium-sharp Cheddar cheese)
3 eggs, separated
½ cup (2 oz/60 g) all-purpose (plain) flour
oil for frying

◼ Roast and peel the *chiles* (see glossary). Make a lengthwise slit in each one, being careful not to break it, and remove the seeds and membranes. Soak the *chiles* in water to cover with 1 tablespoon salt and the vinegar for 20 minutes. Rinse, drain and set aside.

◼ In a blender, purée the tomatoes, onion and garlic, then strain. Heat 1 tablespoon oil in a skillet, add the tomato purée and bring to a boil. Lower the heat, add 1 teaspoon salt, the bay leaves and pepper and cook, covered, for 10 minutes. If the sauce is too thick, thin with up to ¾ cup (6 fl oz/180 ml) of water. Set aside.

◼ Fill each *chile* with ½ cup (2 oz/60 g) of the grated cheese and set aside.

◼ Beat the egg whites until they form stiff peaks, then stir in the yolks one at a time. Spread the flour on a plate, turn each *chile* in it to coat lightly, then dip into the beaten eggs, so that the *chile* is completely coated.

◼ Heat ½ in (1 cm) oil in a skillet. When hot, add the *chiles* one or two at a time and fry on each side until lightly browned. Drain on absorbent paper.

◼ Before serving, heat the tomato sauce and arrange the *chiles* carefully so that each is almost covered with sauce. Cover and simmer for 5 minutes.

Serves 6

Baja California Norte

ENSALADA CESAR
CAESAR SALAD

Caesar salad has had a following ever since the late 1920s, when it was created by two Italian brothers, Alex and Caesar Cardini, in their Tijuana restaurant. It is now featured in many restaurants worldwide, although few versions bear a close resemblance to the original.

2 large heads of romaine (cos) lettuce
5 cloves garlic
1 can (2 oz/56 g) anchovy fillets
3 egg yolks
¼ teaspoon freshly ground pepper
½ teaspoon Maggi (or Worcestershire) sauce
½ teaspoon Worcestershire sauce
¼ cup (2 fl oz/ 60 ml) lime juice
1 cup (8 fl oz/250 ml) plus 2 tablespoons
  olive oil
⅓ cup (1½ oz/45 g) grated Parmesan cheese
12 slices of *bolillo* (hard bread roll) or *baguette*

CAESAR SALAD

▓ Remove the outer leaves from the lettuce; use only the tender centers. Rinse the lettuce, drain and set aside.

▓ Mash the garlic in a mortar or *molcajete*. Place the anchovies in a large bowl and finely shred with a fork. Add the garlic and mix together. Whisk in the egg yolks, then the pepper and the Maggi and Worcestershire sauces. Stir well and add the lime juice. The mixture should be pale yellow in color.

▓ Add the cup of olive oil in a thin stream while whisking constantly. Add 2 tablespoons of the Parmesan cheese.

▓ Heat the remaining oil in a skillet, add the bread slices and fry briefly. Drain and set aside.

▓ To serve, gently toss the lettuce in the dressing and arrange on each plate with 2 slices of fried bread on top. Sprinkle with the remaining cheese and serve immediately.

Serves 6

PANES
Y POSTRES

LITTLE FAMILY-RUN *panaderías* (bakeries) in rural villages are baking the same breads that for generations have satisfied the souls and stomachs of the Mexican people. Made from wheat brought from the Old World and grown in the highlands around Mexico City, the hearty loaves with superb crust were soon considered "as good and cheap as in Spain."

The crusty little rolls called *bolillos* are served in many restaurants, and are also lightly toasted to accompany *huevos rancheros* at the breakfast table. The *telera,* a flatter version of the *bolillo,* is used to make the remarkable *torta,* a many-layered sandwich found in small backstreet restaurants.

The Spanish brought with them their love for *pan dulce.* All sizes and shapes of wonderfully sweet yeast breads are an integral part of the early morning breakfast ritual. Fried fluted fritters called *churros* are another direct descendant from Spain. Christmas Eve is the time for eating *buñuelos,* sweet finger-sticking fritters served in clay dishes. The eve of Epiphany is celebrated with the serving of *rosca de reyes* (ring of the kings), a traditional bread from Spain commemorating the search of the three kings for the baby Jesus. Hidden inside the semi-sweet yeast bread decorated with crystallized fruits is a little doll representing the Christ child.

Magnificent displays of culinary delicacies are traditional on the feast days. A description by one guest, Artemio Valle-Arizpc, in the early 1600s, perhaps best summarizes the variety and abundance of Mexican sweets. He told of "huge platters filled with sugar pastes, delicate almond fruits, royal eggs [egg sponge], pastes made of molasses, cheese, anise and ginger; other trays were covered with milk and honey candies with coconut, as well as almonds fused to resemble pears and apples, coated with liquid caramel and wrapped in colored paper. The silvery bowls were filled to the brim with honey and sugar buns with almonds, sugar and spices, squash preserves, chilacoyes [gourd sweets], transparent candied citrons decorated with sparkling gold and silver confetti, quince candies, marzipan, and almond toffees, toasted or stuffed pears, and sugar-coated peaches, dipped in rum, sparkling like jewels." All of these can still be found today—but not served at the same time!

There is no doubt that the contribution of sweets—whether in the form of breads, candies, or desserts—has been gratefully received into the cuisine of Mexico.

ALMOND CAKE (RECIPE PAGE 109)

MAMEY CAKE

Oaxaca

ANTE DE MAMEY O DURAZNO
MAMEY OR PEACH CAKE

All antes *have a base of cake bread soaked in a syrup, but the paste fillings vary. This version from Socorrito Zorrilla uses the large exotic mamey, with its deep apricot color. It is occasionally sold in some markets outside Mexico.*

1 *marquesote* (opposite page)
⅔ cup (3½ oz/100 g) toasted almonds,
    for garnish
⅔ cup (3½ oz/100 g) toasted pine nuts,
    for garnish

MAMEY OR PEACH PASTE
1¼ cups (10 oz/310 g) sugar
1 cup (8 fl oz/250 ml) water
2 large mameys, peeled and seeded, or
    2 lb (1 kg) peach pulp, puréed
7 tablespoons (3½ oz/100 g) butter

SYRUP
2 cups (1 lb/500 g) sugar
½ cup (4 fl oz/125 ml) water
1 stick cinnamon
2 cups (16 fl oz/500 ml) dry sherry

▦ Remove the crust from the *marquesote*. Slice about ½ in (1 cm) thick and set aside. (If the *marquesote* was baked in a layer cake pan, slice it in half horizontally.)

▦ To make the mamey paste, place the sugar and water in a saucepan and bring to a boil. When the syrup reaches the soft-ball stage (238°F/120°C on a candy thermometer), add the puréed fruit and the butter, lower the heat and beat the mixture until smooth. Set aside.

▦ To make the syrup, mix the sugar, water and cinnamon stick in a heavy saucepan and boil, stirring, until the mixture forms a light syrup. Remove from the heat and stir in the sherry.

▦ Arrange half of the sliced cake bread in a layer on a plate and pour some syrup over it. Spread half of the mamey paste on top and repeat these layers, spreading the mamey paste on top and on all sides. Garnish with the toasted almonds and pine nuts.

Serves 8

Oaxaca

ANTE DE ALMENDRA
ALMOND CAKE

The basic ante, *first made in Puebla, is a cake bread soaked in syrup and mixed with a paste of wine and fruit preserves. Socorrito Zorrilla serves this almond version at her restaurant, El Vitral, in Oaxaca.*

1 *marquesote* (recipe follows)
⅔ cup (3½ oz/100 g) raisins, for garnish
⅔ cup (3½ oz/100 g) toasted almonds,
    for garnish
cinnamon stick, for garnish

ALMOND PASTE
1½ cups (8 oz/250 g) blanched almonds
4 cups (32 fl oz/1 l) milk
1½ cups (12 oz/375 g) sugar

SYRUP
2 cups (1 lb/500 g) sugar
½ cup (4 fl oz/125 ml) water
1 large stick cinnamon
2 cups (16 fl oz/500 ml) dry sherry

Remove the crust from the *marquesote*. Slice about ½ in (1 cm) thick and set aside. (If the *marquesote* was baked in a layer cake pan, slice it in half horizontally.)

To prepare the almond paste, grind the almonds very fine in a nut grinder or mortar. Place in a saucepan with the milk and sugar and boil until thick.

To make the syrup, mix the sugar, water and cinnamon stick in a heavy saucepan and boil, stirring, until the mixture forms a light syrup. Remove from the heat and stir in the sherry.

On a glass plate, arrange half of the sliced cake bread in a layer. Pour some syrup over it and top with half of the almond paste. Repeat these layers, spreading the almond paste on top and on all sides. Garnish with the raisins, toasted almonds and shavings of the cinnamon stick.

Serves 8   *Photograph page 106*

MARQUESOTE
CAKE BREAD

This is one of the classic Mexican cakes, served with just a sprinkle of powdered sugar or as a more elaborate dessert with a wine or fruit syrup (as in ante de almendra). This traditional version was associated with all-male pulquerías, *where it was sold to carousing husbands to take home to placate their jealous wives.*

8 eggs, separated
½ cup (4 oz/125 g) sugar
1 tablespoon baking powder
1½ cups (6 oz/185 g) cornstarch (cornflour)
½ cup (4 oz/125 g) butter, melted
sesame seeds (optional)

Preheat the oven to 375°F (190°C). Grease and flour 2 loaf pans or 9-in (23-cm) square baking pans.

In a large bowl, beat the egg whites until they form stiff peaks. Fold in the yolks one at a time, still beating. Combine the sugar, baking powder and starch. Mix thoroughly. Fold this mixture gently into the eggs and add the melted and cooled butter. Pour into the pans, sprinkle with sesame seeds if you like and bake for about 25 minutes.

Makes 2 Cakes

PATAS
COFFEE BREAD

This rich coffee bread recipe from France has been in the family of Virginia Vázquez for many generations.

3 packages (¼ oz/7 g each) dry yeast
¼ cup (2 fl oz/60 ml) lukewarm water
1½ lb (750 g) all-purpose (plain) flour
4 eggs
⅔ cup (5 oz/155 g) sugar
5 eggs, separated
1½ cups (12 oz/375 g) butter, at room
    temperature
sugar for sprinkling

▓ Dissolve the yeast in the lukewarm water.

▓ Place 2 cups (8 oz/250 g) of the flour in a bowl and make a well in the center. Place 1 egg and 1 tablespoon sugar in the well and add the dissolved yeast. Use the tips of your fingers to combine the ingredients thoroughly. Knead the mixture on a floured board for 10–15 minutes; when you can hear little bubbles popping, the dough is ready.

▓ Place the egg whites in a bowl by the work surface and moisten your hands in them whenever the dough feels dry.

▓ Form the dough into a ball and make a cross on the top surface with a knife. Place in a lightly greased bowl, cover and let stand in a warm place for 1 hour or until it begins to rise.

▓ Place the remaining 4 cups (1 lb/500 g) flour in a large bowl, make a well and add the remaining 3 eggs, the egg yolks and the sugar. With the tips of your fingers, mix half the ingredients in the well with the flour. Add the dough that has been rising and knead all the ingredients together to form a smooth dough. (Moisten your hands with the egg whites whenever necessary and lightly grease the dough with butter whenever it begins to stick.)

▓ Knead for about 30 minutes or until the dough produces small bubbles. Roll it into a cylinder or *baguette* 18 by 2½ in (46 by 6.5 cm); cut the cylinder into 12 slices.

▓ Grease the dough slices with butter. Take one slice and, with the tips of your fingers well greased, stretch it, working outward from the center to the edges, until it measures about 11 in (28 cm) square; it should be transparent. Grease the dough liberally with butter and cut into 3 strips. Wind one of these strips around a greased ¾-in (2-cm) cylinder, such as a cannoli form, a bulb baster or a piece of broom handle. Wind the second strip around the first strip and, finally, the third around the first two (the strips wind continuously, like a roll of tape). Slip this roll onto a greased baking sheet. Repeat the procedure until all the slices have been used up. Be careful to leave 2 in (5 cm) of space between the rolls so they do not stick together.

▓ Place the baking sheets in a warm place, cover the dough and let rise for 3 hours.

▓ Preheat the oven to 350°F (180°C). Sprinkle a tablespoon of sugar on the top of each roll. Bake for 25–30 minutes or until the rolls brown lightly. Remove from the pan and let cool slightly. Serve warm.

Makes 12 Rolls

COFFEE BREAD

140

EMPANADITAS DE HORNO.

A doce libras de harina, veinticinco huevo, cuatro de manteca, una taza otra de agua, sal competente; el mate de esta manera: se frie con todas las espe agua, pero que quede espeso así que se halla mezclado tol bien cocido y se van meterlas en el horno, manteca revuelta co ajonjolí.

SUGAR-COATED FRIED BREAD

TORREJAS

SUGAR-COATED FRIED BREAD

In the state of Puebla it is customary to feed children this Mexican version of French toast when they get their first tooth.

3 cups (24 fl oz/750 ml) milk
1 3-in (7.5-cm) stick cinnamon

½ cup (4 oz/125 g) sugar or grated *piloncillo* (raw sugar)
14 ½-in (1-cm) slices *bolillo* (hard bread roll) or *baguette*
oil for frying
4 eggs, lightly beaten

SYRUP
2 cups (16 fl oz/500 ml) water
1 2-in (5-cm) stick cinnamon

2 cups (1 lb/500 g) grated *piloncillo* (raw sugar)
or brown sugar
1 tablespoon fine julienne strips of lime peel

▦ Place the milk, cinnamon and sugar in a heavy saucepan and boil for 5 minutes. Let cool.

▦ Place the bread slices in a large baking dish. Cover with 2 cups (16 fl oz/500 ml) of the boiled milk and let stand for 1 hour.

▦ Meanwhile, prepare the syrup. Mix the water, cinnamon, *piloncillo* and lime peel in a saucepan and boil until the *piloncillo* dissolves and the mixture thickens slightly. Set aside and keep warm.

▦ Heat ½ in (1 cm) oil in a skillet. Dip the soaked bread in the beaten eggs and place in the hot oil. Fry for 2–3 minutes on each side or until golden brown. Transfer to a platter. Serve the fritters covered with the *piloncillo* syrup or sprinkled with white sugar.

Serves 6

Puebla

POLVORONES DE NARANJA
ORANGE "DUSTS"

Each part of Mexico has its own version of these flaky cookies, which take their name from the word polvo *(dust), referring to their light consistency. María Dolores Torres Yzábal uses orange for flavoring, but ground nuts and cinnamon are also common. A mix of half butter and half vegetable shortening can be substituted for the lard.*

1 cup (8 oz/250 g) lard
½ cup (4 oz/125 g) sugar
2 large egg yolks

¼ cup (2 fl oz/60 ml) orange juice
peel of 2 oranges, grated
4 cups (1 lb/500 g) all-purpose (plain) flour
powdered (icing) sugar

▦ Preheat the oven to 400°F (200°C). In a large bowl, beat the lard until it is fluffy. Add the sugar a little at a time. When it is thoroughly mixed in, add the egg yolks, orange juice and orange peel. Stir in the flour with a spatula.

▦ On a floured surface, roll out the dough to a thickness of ¾ in (2 cm). Cut out 2½-in (6-cm) circles and place them on a greased baking sheet. Reroll the scraps and continue until all of the dough has been used.

▦ Bake for 25 minutes or until the cookies begin to brown lightly around the edges. Transfer to a rack to cool, then arrange on a platter and sprinkle with the sugar through a fine sieve.

Makes 36 Cookies

ORANGE "DUSTS"

FLAN BLANCO
WHITE FLAN

While this is not a flan in the traditional sense—it is missing two of the custard's main ingredients, egg yolks and milk— it has flan's caramel coating, with the added surprise of a light meringue-type filling. This recipe is by Rosario Madero, who shares it with her family at their Chihuahua hacienda.

12 egg whites
⅛ teaspoon salt
½ teaspoon cream of tartar
¾–1 cup (6–8 oz/185–250 g) sugar
1½ teaspoons vanilla extract (essence)
½ teaspoon almond extract (essence)

CARAMEL
1½ cups (12 oz/375 g) sugar
⅛ teaspoon salt
½ teaspoon vanilla extract (essence)
¼ teaspoon almond extract (essence)

TOPPING
1 cup (8 fl oz/250 ml) heavy (double) cream
pinch of salt
1 tablespoon powdered (icing) sugar
½ teaspoon vanilla extract (essence)
¼ teaspoon almond extract (essence)
1 cup (5 oz/155 g) toasted blanched almond
    halves, for garnish

☒ Preheat the oven to 350°F (180°C). Place the ingredients for the caramel in a heavy saucepan over medium heat. Swirl the pan constantly until the sugar melts and caramelizes, turning a light golden brown. Pour into a 2-qt (2-l) ring mold or Bundt pan and tilt so that the caramel covers the bottom and sides. Set aside.

☒ Place the egg whites in a large bowl, add the salt and cream of tartar and beat until the whites form stiff peaks. Fold in the sugar, then add the extracts. Pour this mixture into the caramel-coated mold (the caramel should be hard by this time). Set the mold in a larger pan and pour 1 in (2.5 cm) boiling water into the pan. Place in the oven and bake for 45–60 minutes. Do not remove the mold from the oven immediately; instead, turn off the oven

WHITE FLAN (LEFT) AND COFFEE GELATIN (RIGHT, RECIPE PAGE 117)

and leave the mold in the oven with the door open for 10 minutes before taking it out. Then be careful to put the mold in a spot where there are no drafts or extreme temperature changes.

When the mold cools to room temperature (about 20 minutes), unmold the *flan* onto a platter and cover with the caramel sauce. To remove any caramel that sticks to the mold, place 1 cup (8 fl oz/250 ml) water in the mold and hold it over a hot burner on the stove, stirring until the caramel is loosened; let cool a little and pour the diluted caramel over the *flan*.

To prepare the topping, beat the cream with a pinch of salt. When it begins to thicken, mix in the sugar and the extracts. Beat until stiff. Spoon dollops of cream onto the *flan* and garnish with the toasted almond halves.

Serves 8

CARAMEL CRÊPES

CREPAS DE CAJETA
CARAMEL CRÊPES

The original rich-tasting goat's milk cajeta was sold in little wooden cajas (boxes) in the shops of Celaya, Guanajuato, where it was made in huge copper pots. Today it is more commonly sold in glass jars in different flavors and can be used as a dessert topping, as in this recipe for crêpes.

CRÊPES
1½ cups (12 fl oz/375 ml) milk
½ cup (2 oz/60 g) all-purpose (plain) flour
1 egg
1 tablespoon oil
butter

SAUCE
2 tablespoons (1 oz/30 g) butter
1 cup (8 fl oz/250 ml) *cajeta* (recipe follows)
½ cup (4 fl oz/125 ml) orange juice
1 tablespoon white tequila
¾ cup (3 oz/90 g) chopped walnuts

To prepare the crêpes, beat the milk, flour, egg and oil together in a mixing bowl. Let rest for 5 minutes. Lightly butter a nonstick crêpe pan and set over medium heat. Pour 1½ tablespoons of the mixture into the pan and tilt it to cover the bottom. As soon as the edges of the crêpe begin to dry out, turn it over. When the second side is lightly browned, transfer the crêpe to a plate. Repeat until all the mixture has been used, being sure to butter the pan before making each crêpe. There should be about 12 crêpes. Set aside.

To prepare the sauce, melt the butter in a small saucepan and add the *cajeta* and orange juice. Stir over medium heat for 3–5 minutes or until heated and thoroughly combined. Add the tequila, heat, ignite and let burn off.

🔲 Before serving, briefly heat the sauce. Fold each crêpe in half, then fold again to make a triangle. Dip each of the crêpes in the sauce. Place 2 crêpes on each plate and divide the remaining sauce among the 6 plates. Sprinkle with the chopped walnuts. Serve hot.

Serves 6

CAJETA

CARAMEL SAUCE

¼ cup (2 fl oz/60 ml) water
1 teaspoon baking soda (bicarbonate of soda)
4 cups (32 fl oz/1 l) milk (preferably goat's milk)
1 cup (8 oz/250 g) sugar
1 teaspoon vanilla extract (essence) (optional)

🔲 In a cup, stir the water and baking soda together. Set aside.

🔲 Stir the milk and sugar together in a saucepan and bring to a boil. Lower the heat to medium and, stirring constantly, pour in the baking soda water in a thin stream; be careful not to let any baking soda sitting in the bottom of the cup be poured in. Continue cooking and stirring for 50–60 minutes or until the mixture coats the back of a spoon, turns a rich caramel color and is clear.

🔲 Pour the mixture into a bowl, stir in the vanilla and let cool. The *cajeta* can be made 1 or 2 months in advance, covered and refrigerated.

Makes about 3½ cups (28 fl oz/875 ml)

GELATINA DE CAFÉ CON LICOR DE CAFÉ
COFFEE GELATIN

Gelatins are extremely popular in Mexico—served in a rainbow of colors or made with milk and fruits. This dessert pays homage to the coffee liqueurs of Mexico, now esteemed in many countries. It is an ideal elegant ending to a rich main course.

1 package (2½ teaspoons) unflavored gelatin
1½ cups (12 fl oz/375 ml) cold water
¼ cup (2 oz/60 g) sugar
3 teaspoons instant coffee granules
1 cup (8 fl oz/250 ml) Kahlua or other coffee liqueur

🔲 In a small bowl, sprinkle the gelatin over ½ cup (4 fl oz/125 ml) of the water and let stand for 5 minutes or until absorbed.

🔲 Meanwhile, place the remaining water and the sugar and instant coffee in a saucepan over medium heat. Cook, stirring, until the sugar dissolves. When the mixture begins to boil, remove from the heat. Add the gelatin and stir until it dissolves. Add the coffee liqueur and stir to combine.

🔲 Pour the mixture into lightly greased individual molds or into a lightly greased 4-cup (1½-pt/1-l) mold. Let cool slightly and refrigerate for 3 hours or until the gelatin is firm. Unmold the gelatin and garnish each serving with a dollop of whipped cream, a maraschino cherry and a mint leaf. Or garnish with chocolate shavings or a coffee bean.

Serves 6   *Photograph pages 114–115*

FLAN
CARAMEL CUSTARD

This universally known Spanish dessert is also a favorite in Mexico, tracing its origin here to the days of the Conquest, when milk and eggs were introduced by the Spaniards. Egg custards are popular in many cuisines, but the signature of the flan *is its caramelized sugar topping. This basic recipe can be contemporized by adding 2 tablespoons of instant coffee and 2 teaspoons of coffee liqueur.*

1¼ cups (10 oz/310 g) sugar
4 cups (32 fl oz/1 l) milk
1 teaspoon vanilla extract (essence)
pinch of salt
4 eggs
3 egg yolks
½ teaspoon cornstarch (cornflour)
1 tablespoon cold water

▨ Preheat the oven to 350°F (180°C). Place ¾ cup (6 oz/ 185 g) of the sugar in a heavy saucepan over medium heat. Swirl the pan constantly until the sugar melts and caramelizes, turning a golden brown. Pour into a 1½-qt (1.5-l) ring mold, Charlotte mold or round baking dish and tilt the mold so that the caramel covers the bottom and sides. Set aside.

▨ In a separate saucepan, combine the milk, remaining ½ cup (4 oz/125 g) sugar, vanilla and salt and bring to a boil. Lower the heat and simmer, uncovered, for 10 minutes or until the milk is reduced by half. Cover to keep warm and set aside.

▨ Lightly beat the eggs and egg yolks in a large bowl. Stir the cornstarch and water together and add to the eggs. Slowly pour in the warm milk, stirring constantly. Mix well, strain and pour into the caramel-coated mold.

▨ Cover the mold with foil, set in a larger pan and pour 1 in (2.5 cm) boiling water into the pan. Place in the oven and bake for 35–40 minutes or until a knife inserted near the center comes out clean.

▨ Let the *flan* cool for 30 minutes to room temperature and then refrigerate, preferably overnight. To serve, invert the mold on a platter. Serve cold.

▨ *Note:* If the caramel has hardened on the bottom of the mold, quickly place it in a pan of hot water to soften.

Serves 6

Yucatán

TORTA IMPERIAL
IMPERIAL TORTE

This light cake is representative of the European influence in Mérida during the period of colonization.

2 cups (10 oz/315 g) blanched almonds
1 tablespoon all-purpose (plain) flour
6 eggs, separated
1 teaspoon cream of tartar
1¾ cups (14 oz/435 g) sugar
½ teaspoon vanilla extract (essence)
2 cups (16 fl oz/500 ml) water
1 3-in (7.5-cm) stick cinnamon
1 tablespoon grated orange peel
1 teaspoon orange liqueur
¼ cup (1 oz/30 g) toasted chopped almonds

CARAMEL CUSTARD (LEFT) AND IMPERIAL TORTE (RIGHT)

▦ Preheat the oven to 325°F (165°C). Grease and flour a 9-in (23-cm) springform pan (cake tin).

▦ In a nut grinder or food processor, grind the almonds. Mix with the flour and set aside.

▦ In a large bowl, beat the egg whites until frothy. Add the cream of tartar and continue beating, adding 1 cup (8 oz/250 g) of the sugar, 1 tablespoon at a time, until the whites hold stiff peaks. Add the yolks one at a time, then the vanilla. Fold in the almond-flour mixture with a spatula. Transfer the batter to the prepared pan and bake for 25–35 minutes. Let cool for 5 minutes, unmold and set aside.

▦ Heat the water with the remaining ¾ cup (6 oz/185 g) sugar and the cinnamon stick and orange peel. Cook over medium heat until the mixture thickens slightly. Stir in the orange liqueur and pour over the torte. Sprinkle with the toasted almonds and serve.

▦ *Variation:* The torte can be covered with a custard or pastry cream instead of the syrup.

Serves 6

ROYAL EGGS

Puebla

HUEVOS REALES

ROYAL EGGS

Like mole poblano, *this very sweet dish is attributed to the creative Dominican nuns of the Santa Rosa convent. Egg whites were used to paint the walls of the convent, and it is said that* huevos reales *were dreamed up as a way to use the remaining yolks. It can be prepared a day in advance.*

10 egg yolks
2 teaspoons baking powder
1 teaspoon butter

⅓ cup (2 oz/60 g) raisins, for garnish
cinnamon shavings, for garnish

SYRUP
2 cups (16 oz/500 g) sugar
1 cup (8 fl oz/250 ml) water
7 1-in (2.5-cm) sticks cinnamon
2 tablespoons dry sherry

❧ Preheat the oven to 275°F (135°C). In a large bowl, beat the egg yolks until they are thick and creamy. Stir in the baking powder. ❧ Grease a 13- by 9-in (33- by 23-cm) baking dish with the butter and pour in the egg

120

mixture. Cover the dish with aluminum foil and bake for about 45 minutes or until a toothpick inserted in the center comes out clean (be careful not to overbake). Remove from the oven and let cool for 10 minutes.

To make the syrup, mix the sugar, water and cinnamon in a small heavy saucepan and boil, stirring, for 5 minutes until the mixture forms a light syrup. Remove from the heat and stir in the sherry.

Cut the eggs in the baking dish into 1-in (2.5-cm) squares. Cover with the syrup and garnish with raisins and cinnamon shavings. Serve chilled or at room temperature.

Serves 8

ARROZ CON LECHE
RICE PUDDING

Rice pudding, the most loved of all Mexican desserts, is found in virtually every marketplace and restaurant in Mexico. A tablespoon of brandy can be added for a special occasion. It is delicious served at any temperature—chilled, warm or room temperature.

1 cup (5 oz/155 g) long-grain white rice
3 cups (24 fl oz/750 ml) water
1 3-in (7.5-cm) stick cinnamon
1 tablespoon very fine julienne strips of lime
   or orange peel (optional)
pinch of salt
4 cups (32 fl oz/1 l) milk
1½ cups (12 oz/375 g) sugar or to taste
⅓ cup (2 oz/60 g) raisins
1 teaspoon vanilla extract (essence)
ground cinnamon, for garnish (optional)

Place the rice in a large saucepan with the water, cinnamon, lime peel and salt. Bring to a boil, lower the heat and cook, covered, until most of the water has been absorbed. Stir in the milk and sugar and cook, stirring constantly, over low heat until the mixture thickens. Add the raisins and vanilla and cook for 2 minutes. Remove from the heat and let cool for 20 minutes. Transfer to a platter or individual bowls and refrigerate. Sprinkle lightly with cinnamon before serving.

Variation: For a richer, more custard-like flavor, beat an egg into the milk before adding it to the pan.

Serves 6

RICE PUDDING

GLOSSARY

It is always frustrating to find an enticing recipe and then realize that the essential ingredients may not be available. This may be true of many of the recipes in this book, so substitutes have been suggested whenever possible. Many of these ingredients can be found in Hispanic or Asian markets, and more and more they are being carried in ordinary supermarkets. All of the recipes in this book were tested in home kitchens throughout the United States with locally obtained ingredients.

ACHIOTE: The deep red-orange seeds of the tropical *annatto* tree are used in the Yucatán both for their distinctive flavor and their brilliant yellow color, which is used commercially to color cheese. Both the seeds (often labeled *annatto*) and a flavorful paste are available in Latin American and specialty food shops.

AVOCADO/AGUACATE: A deciduous tree of the Lauracea family, which is native to Mexico, bears a fruit with a leathery skin, a large seed and soft, buttery flesh. There are many varieties of avocados—from little fingerlike ones that are eaten skin and all, to a giant pear-shaped avocado with a reddish-tinged skin. The best known outside Mexico is the almost smooth, green-skinned Fuerte, which has a bland taste, and the dark, knobby-skinned Hass, with its wonderful, nutty flavor. The other, bigger varieties that occasionally appear in grocery stores can have a stringy texture. To ripen an avocado, seal it in a paper bag at room temperature. It can then be stored in the refrigerator. The long leathery leaves are used in some dishes. Their characteristic flavor is only found in the leaves of mature trees, so ask your friends who live where they are grown to send you a supply, as dried leaves can be used in most recipes.

BANANA LEAVES: In southern Mexico, the Yucatán and the Gulf states, the large, fragrant leaves of the banana plant are used to wrap food for cooking and to impart flavor. They can be found frozen in most Latin and Asian markets. Thaw by quickly passing the leaf over a flame or steam to make it more pliable.

BOLILLOS: Small, crusty, French-type bread rolls with an oblong shape.

BUDÍN: This almost cakelike pudding is usually made from vegetables. It is served for a light supper or as a *sopa seca* (dry soup) during a large *comida* (main meal of the day).

CAZUELA: This traditional earthenware casserole of Mexico, glazed on the inside and rough on the outside, is used for *moles* and stews, as it heats evenly and retains heat for a long time. A *cazuelita* is small *cazuela* or ramekin.

CHEESES: Some of these cheeses are hard to find even in Mexico because they are regional.

QUESO AÑEJO: A dry, salty cheese that is finely grated and used as a tasty garnish. Romano can be used as a substitute.

QUESO ASADERO: A mild, soft, braided cheese used for dishes requiring melted cheese. Provolone, mozzarella, Monterey Jack or block Muenster can be substituted.

QUESO CHIHUAHUA: A mild, nutty-tasting cheese. Monterey Jack or a medium-sharp Cheddar is a good substitute.

QUESO FRESCO: A tangy, crumbly cheese. Feta is about the best substitute.

QUESO MANCHEGO: Similar to the original sheep cheeses of Spain and varies considerably in flavor and consistency. Substitute a young pecorino, table Parmesan or raw-milk Cheddar.

QUESO PANELA: A porous fresh cheese from central Mexico. A fresh mozzarella is the closest substitute.

CHAYOTE: Also called vegetable pear, choko, christophene or mirliton, this pear-shaped vegetable is a member of the squash family. Three varieties are found in Mexico, the best tasting being dark green with porcupine-like spines. The pale *chayote* found in U.S. markets is rather tasteless and needs more seasoning. It stores well unwrapped in the refrigerator for up to a month. The flavor is reminiscent of its cucumber relative.

CHILES
The many *chiles* all belong to the genus *Capsicum* and vary in degree of hotness and in flavor, not only between species but between plants of the same species, depending on such variables as soil and climate. To

confuse things even more, the same *chiles* may go by different names in the different states of Mexico. Wearing rubber gloves is a good idea when preparing *chiles,* as the pithy white placenta, or seed cluster, can burn the skin. Be careful not to touch your eyes.

CHILES FRESCOS (FRESH CHILES)

The fat, dark green *chile jalapeño,* named after the capital of Veracruz, is the most common *chile* used in Mexican cooking, along with the smaller *chile serrano.* Both of these hot *chiles* are eaten pickled or fresh in uncooked *salsas* and *guacamole.* The *chile cuaresmeño* of the central region is the same as the *jalapeño.* The *chile poblano* is larger and much milder than the *jalapeño,* and is best known for making *chiles rellenos.* The Anaheim or unnamed long green peppers in the supermarkets are marginal substitutes. The *chile güero* or blond *chile* is any very light yellow or pale green *chile.* A Fresno *chile,* the long yellow banana or Hungarian wax pepper, or even a *jalapeño* can be substituted.

TO ROAST FRESH CHILES:

Chiles are roasted in order to remove the thin skin that covers them as well as to give them a unique flavor. There are several methods:

1. Over direct heat

Place the *chiles* directly over a medium flame on a gas stove. Turn the *chiles* with tongs until their entire skins are "charred" (covered with black blisters). This will take 5–10 minutes, depending on the heat of the flame and the size of the *chiles.* Do not char the *chiles* too much or the flesh will burn and taste bitter. Immediately place the *chiles* in a plastic bag and close the bag. Or cover the *chiles* with a damp cloth. Leave for 10–15 minutes to "sweat." This procedure makes the thin skin easier to remove and lets the *chiles* cook slightly in their own steam.

2. On a *comal*

If you don't have a *comal,* use a heavy iron or nonstick skillet (frying pan). Heat the *comal* over medium heat. Place 2 or 3 *chiles* at a time on it and cook, turning, until the entire skin of each *chile* is "charred" (covered with black blisters). This will take 10–15 minutes. Place in a bag and allow to "sweat" as described above.

3. In a broiler

Heat the broiler (griller) to medium-high heat. Lightly brush each *chile* with oil. Place all the *chiles* in the pan and put it in the broiler. Broil, turning the *chiles,* until their entire skins are "charred." This will take 10–15 minutes. Place in a bag and allow to "sweat" as described above.

4. In oil

This method saves a lot of time and labor in peeling large quantities of *chiles.* Heat a cup of oil over medium-high heat in a skillet. Add the chiles 1 or 2 at a time. Use a spatula or a slotted spoon to turn the *chiles* and fry them until their skins swell and turn golden brown, 5–10 seconds. Transfer the *chiles* to a bowl containing cold water and use your fingers to peel off the thin skins.

TO PEEL CHILES:

Hold each *chile* under a thin stream of cold running water and use your fingers to remove the charred skins. If parts of the skin stick to the *chile,* use a paring knife to remove them. Or you can dip the *chiles* in a medium-sized bowl full of water as needed to peel each *chile.* Do not let them soak or they will lose flavor.

TO REMOVE THE MEMBRANES AND SEEDS:

If the *chile* is to be used whole and stuffed, do not remove the stem and be careful not to break the skin while cleaning the *chile.* Use a small knife and carefully make a lateral incision in the *chile;* remove the placenta, which is the small cluster of seeds attached to the base of the stem; also remove the membranes that run the length of the *chile.* Gently rinse the *chile* to remove any seeds that are still adhering to it.

If the *chile* is to be cut into strips, cut a "lid" in the top part of the *chile,* by the stem, and remove. Make a lateral incision in the *chile,* pull open and remove the seeds and membranes. Rinse the *chile* and cut it into strips.

TO SOAK FRESH CHILES:

Submerge *chiles* in a mixture of 1 cup (8 fl oz/250 ml) water, 1 tablespoon white vinegar, and 2 teaspoons salt (double or triple the quantities depending on the number of *chiles*). The purpose of soaking is to remove excess piquancy. If the *chiles* are too fiery, it may be necessary to let them soak for a little while; 40 minutes is usually long enough. After soaking, rinse the *chiles* briefly.

CHILES SECOS (DRIED CHILES)

The *chile ancho,* or "wide" *chile,* is the dried form of the *chile poblano* and is also commonly used, mainly as a base for sauces. It has a bittersweet flavor and the aroma of prunes. The *chile mulato* has a full, almost bitter taste. The long, narrow, wrinkled *chile pasilla* has a rich, very *picante* flavor and it is used extensively in *moles,* sauces and as a garnish for soup. Fresh, it is the *chile chilaca.* The other commonly used dried *chile,* the *guajillo,* looks like its Spanish name, which means "old dried thing." After soaking and grinding, it is used to spice up various meals and stews. It is quite hot and has an uncomplicated *chile* taste. The tiny, very hot *chile pequín* or *piquín* is often ground. The *chile chipotle* is the light brown smoked *chile jalapeño,* which is usually canned in *adobo* sauce or in vinegar but is also found dried and smoked, as is the similar *chile morita,* which is more triangular. Both have a very distinctive smoky smell and taste. The small, round *chile cascabel* sounds like a rattle when it is shaken. It adds a hot, nutty flavor to table *salsas.*

TO CLEAN DRIED CHILES:
Wipe the skin of the *chile* with a damp cloth to remove any impurities. Follow instructions above for removing membranes and seeds. Sometimes *chiles* are too dry, and when you try to remove the seeds and membranes, they break into small pieces. If that happens, toast and soak the *chiles* before cleaning them.

TO ROAST OR TOAST DRIED CHILES:
Heat a *comal* or iron skillet over medium heat. Place the *chiles* in the hot skillet, using a spatula to press them against it slightly. Turn them so that both sides begin to change color. This will take 1–2 minutes. Be careful not to burn them.

TO SOAK DRIED CHILES:
Place the *chiles* in just enough lukewarm or hot water to cover for 5–10 minutes; this softens them and makes them regain body.

TO FRY DRIED CHILES:
Heat a scant tablespoon of oil in a small skillet. Add the *chile* and fry lightly for a minute. If a crisper *chile* is desired, fry it over medium heat for 3–4 minutes, turning constantly so that it doesn't burn.

CHORIZO: This wonderfully fragrant sausage is made of sections of pig intestine stuffed with a seasoned ground pork mixture. Usually sold in links, it is more highly seasoned than Spanish *chorizo.* While quite good *chorizo* may be purchased at many meat markets, stay clear of the plastic-wrapped mixtures seen at some supermarkets. *Chorizo* must be cooked before eating. If not available, Polish kielbasa, Cajun smoked Andouille or similar spicy pork sausage could be substituted.

CILANTRO (*Coriandrum sativum*): Also known as coriander or Chinese parsley, this herb has a distinctive flavor that makes it indispensable in Mexican cooking. It is sold with its roots and should be stored in the refrigerator, standing in a glass of water and lightly covered with a plastic bag or wrap.

COMAL: This thin, unglazed clay or metal circular plate is placed over heat and used to cook or heat tortillas and other foods. A cast-iron skillet (frying pan) or griddle can be used.

CREAM: Sweet cream is available and usually whipped for desserts, but when recipes call for cream, it is usually a thick, slightly sour cream similar to *crème fraîche* that is wanted. To make, stir 2 tablespoons sour cream, buttermilk or plain yogurt into 1 cup heavy (double) cream, cover and let stand in a warm place until thickened (8–24 hours). Stir and refrigerate. It will keep for up to a week. The best flavor develops if allowed to age in the refrigerator for several days. Commercial sour cream is not a good substitute because of its lower butterfat content, which causes it to curdle when brought to a boil.

CUITLACOCHE: Often spelled *huitlacoche,* this fungus grows on ears of corn and is commonly used in central Mexico in soups, crêpes and other dishes. Although *cuitlacoche* has been considered a delicacy in Mexico for centuries, it is only now becoming sought after by chefs in the rest of the world. It is found wherever corn is grown but is usually destroyed. Fresh *cuitlacoche* is not generally available commercially outside Mexico, but most corn farmers will gladly give you their corn "smut." It is sometimes found canned in Latin American markets.

Epazote (Chenopodium ambrosioides): This pungent annual herb, which may be indigenous to Mexico, has no substitute for its unusual flavor, which is almost a prerequisite in a pot of black beans. Although seldom available commercially outside Mexico, except in India, it is easily grown from seed and quickly self-propagates. Also known as goosefoot or wormseed, it is considered a weed in most other countries. Both seeds and plants are available from some specialty plant catalogs. It can be used dried, after the twigs are discarded, but the flavor is greatly diminished.

Flor de Calabaza/Squash Blossom: The large male flower of certain varieties of hard-skinned squash or zucchini is lightly steamed for use in various dishes. They should be used the day they are picked. They can be found fresh in season at some greengrocers or canned in Latin American grocery stores.

Frijoles/Beans: There are many varieties of dried beans grown in Mexico. The most common are the small black turtle beans of southeast Mexico and the Gulf coast; the fancifully named purple *flor de mayo* and the biscuit-colored *bayos* most often found in the central region; and the speckled pinto, the bean of choice in northern Mexico.

Hierba Buena (Mentha spicata and other species): Also spelled *yerba buena,* this is mint, or literally "good herb."

Hierba Santa (Piper sanctum): Also called *hoya santa,* this large, soft-leaved herb has a strong anise flavor that is much prized in Oaxaca, Chiapas, Tabasco and Veracruz.

Hominy/Cacahuazintle: Dried corn kernels are cooked with powdered lime (calcium oxide) until the skins slip off and further simmered until they open up like a flower. Hominy is used in Mexico for *pozole* and some versions of *menudo* and other soups. Canned hominy can be used but does not have the same texture.

Huachinango/Red Snapper: This magnificent Gulf coast fish is excellent cut into steaks and fillets. Those under 5 pounds are often prepared whole. On the Pacific a smaller, very red species is marketed. Both are quite plentiful and delicious.

Jícama: Indigenous to Mexico, this light brown, bulbous tuber with a crisp ivory flesh (also known as a yam bean) is comparable to a water chestnut. It is usually eaten raw with a squirt of lime, a little salt and ground *chile.* It keeps a long time in the refrigerator if whole. It is generally available year-round in grocery stores.

Lard/Manteca de Cerdo: The rendered fat of the pig is the traditional cooking fat of Mexico but is truly essential only in a few dishes. Lard has one-half the cholesterol of butter. It is important to use "real" lard, not the processed hydrogenated kind sold in most supermarkets. It is easy to render your own: Grind up small pieces of fat in a food processor, place in a roasting pan in a 250°F (130°C) oven until melted. Strain and store in the refrigerator.

Mamey: This large, oval-shaped tropical fruit has a rich, rose-peach flesh and brown leathery skin. It is usually eaten raw.

Masa: This corn dough, made from treated ground field corn and water, can be purchased fresh or frozen from tortilla "factories" in major cities. It spoils quickly, so use within a day if fresh or thawed.

Masa Harina: This dried corn flour, found in many supermarkets, can be used as an adequate alternative to fresh *masa.* It is not the same as cornmeal. The most common and reliable brand is Quaker.

Metate y Mano: These centuries-old implements made of basalt are used to grind corn, *chiles,* cacao and other ingredients. Traditional Indian cooks still kneel on the ground, rolling the cylindrical *mano* over the slanting three-legged table-like *metate.*

Molcajete y Tejolote: A three-legged basalt mortar and pestle used to grind spices and ingredients for fresh *salsas.*

Mole: A Náhuatl word describing a sauce or mixture containing *chile.* There are many variations, only a few containing chocolate.

Nopales: The flat-jointed paddles of the prickly pear, or nopal cactus. They are prized for food, as are the juicy fruits. Fresh *nopales* are now found in Mexican markets, and the bottled or canned *nopalitos* are available in some specialty and Latin American stores in other parts of the world. Be careful when working with fresh whole *nopales,* as they have very sharp thorns that must be removed before cooking. It is best to wear gloves. Hold by the base and, with a very sharp knife, shave off the bumps that contain the thorns, but do not remove the entire outer skin. Cut off the thick base and trim the edges of the paddle. Rinse and cut into ½-in (1-cm) squares. Add a handful of green (spring) onion tops to a pot of boiling salted water, then add the *nopales.* Boil until tender, about 10 minutes. Drain and rinse thoroughly in cold water to remove the sticky substance that is released from the cactus.

OLLA: A large-necked clay pot with two handles used for cooking beans, stews, soups and similar dishes. It must be cured before using.

PILONCILLO: Most commonly shaped into hard cones, *piloncillo* is unrefined sugar. It is grated or chopped for use. It can be found in most Latin American markets, or dark brown sugar may be substituted.

RECADOS: These seasoning pastes are used primarily in the Yucatán and Central America. The best known contains a mixture of *achiote* and other herbs and spices. They are found prepared in small balls or oblong packages in Latin American markets or can be made at home (see recipe on page 67).

ROASTING: See *Chiles Frescos* for instructions on roasting *chiles.* A similar technique *(asar)* is used to roast or grill onions, garlic and tomatoes.

> *ONIONS/GARLIC:* Cook on a *comal* or griddle over medium-high heat until outer layer is charred, turning as needed. The dried outer skin is usually removed first.

> *TOMATOES:* Place the tomatoes on a *comal* or griddle and grill until the skin is charred. Or, put the tomatoes in a baking pan lined with foil and broil until skin is blackened, turning once.

ROBALO/SNOOK: A popular Gulf coast fish that is prepared like red snapper. A similar species is found in Pacific waters.

TAMAL: Masa mixed with lard, spread on corn husks or banana leaves, sometimes with a savory filling, then wrapped and steamed. There are a vast number of sizes, shapes and tastes of *tamales,* even sweet ones. They are usually served as a meal in themselves and usually on festive occasions. Any extras freeze very well and can be reheated by covering in foil and baking in a moderate oven (325°F/160°C) until thawed and heated through.

TOASTING: See *Chiles Secos* for instructions on toasting *chiles.* A similar technique can be used for nuts, seeds and spices. Just toast them lightly on a hot *comal* or small cast-iron skillet until their fragrance is released. The seeds will pop, so be careful.

TOMATE VERDE: Also called *tomatillo* or *miltomate* in some regions, this is not a green tomato but a relative of the gooseberry, with a small fruit covered by a parchment-like calyx. An important ingredient in many Mexican dishes, it is now found in many supermarkets outside Mexico. It also is available canned.

TORTILLA: A thin round of ground dried corn made into dough *(masa)* and quickly cooked on a *comal.* It serves as the bread of Mexico—as a wrapper, an edible scoop and a plate. (To make your own tortillas, see the recipe on page 15.) Most tortillas are white or yellow. In the villages you can even find red or blue tortillas made from wild corn. In northern Mexico wheat-flour tortillas are common, but for most Mexicans, the word tortilla means a tortilla made with corn *masa.*

TORTILLA PRESS: Cast-iron tortilla presses are available in Mexican grocery stores and some specialty kitchen stores. Avoid purchasing the lighter aluminum ones. In Mexico, there are also presses made of wood.

VANILLA: This flavoring is obtained from the cured dried pods of a perennial orchid that twists and climbs its way to the tops of trees in the humid tropical forests of Veracruz. Each long, narrow, shriveled black pod contains thousands of very small seeds, the source of the flavor. Though whole pods are expensive, they can be washed off and reused many times. Because much of the liquid vanilla from Mexico contains a synthetic flavor that can be harmful in large amounts, it is banned in the United States. When bringing bottles back from Mexico, always make sure they contain pure vanilla extract.

INDEX